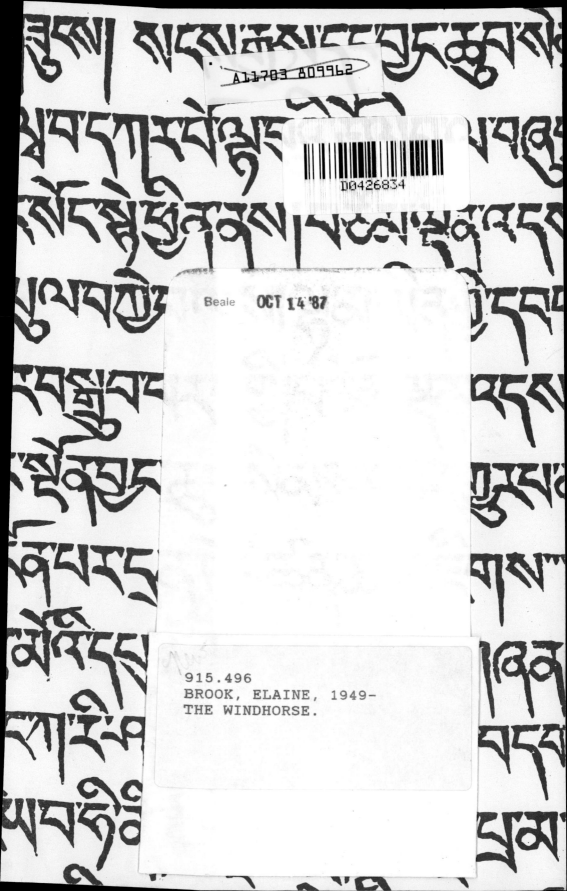

The Windhorse

The Windhorse

Elaine Brook
and
Julie Donnelly

DODD, MEAD & COMPANY
NEW YORK

First published in the United States in 1987
Copyright © 1986 by Elaine Brook

Published by Dodd, Mead & Company, Inc.
71 Fifth Avenue, New York, N.Y. 10003

Manufactured in Great Britain

Originally published in Great Britain by Jonathan Cape Ltd.

First Edition

ISBN 0-396-09006-0

To Isabel and Alec,
Mona and Alfred,
whose love and support
made our journey possible

Contents

Illustrations

Photographs by Elaine Brook, with the exception of Julie as a child, taken by her father, Elaine solo rock-climbing by Richard Pitman, Judy Sterner's picture of Elaine climbing in Bolivia, Julie rock-climbing in Derbyshire by Peter Hatton, Lhakpa Sherpa's photographs of Elaine in Nepal and Mingmar's of Julie, Elaine and Lhakpa at the summit of Kala Patthar.

Decorations

The windhorse on page 13 is taken from Tapkhay's prayer flag, which is reproduced in full on page 62. Part of the Tibetan script from the flag has been enlarged for the book's endpapers. The eight auspicious signs round the border represent rare and precious offerings to the Buddhas, high lamas and kings, and are used as chapter-title decorations in the following order for chapters 1 to 8 and in reverse order for chapters 9 to 16:

1 The precious umbrella or parasol, adorned with jewels, is held above the head of a spiritual leader or king. It keeps away the heat of the sun and so symbolises a protection from delusions of the mind.
2 The lotus grows from a muddy swamp, yet opens as a beautiful and pure flower. It symbolises the potential purity of the human mind.
3 The knot of eternity symbolises the indestructible quality of meditation and its realisation of the ultimate nature.
4 The golden wheel of Dharma symbolises the Buddha's religious teaching which brings peace and harmony.
5 The golden fish symbolises one who has crossed the ocean of worldly existence to attain Buddhahood.

6 The vase is filled with treasure and symbolises the fulfilment of spiritual desires.

7 The banner symbolises victory over obstacles and negative
states of mind.

8 The rightward-turning and most rare conch symbolises
the declaration of the Buddha's teachings to all world
beings. The sound of the conch when blown travels a great
distance.

I am the Windhorse!
I am the king of space, the master of infinity,
Traversing the universe
With flashing, fiery hooves!
On my strong back, on a saddle blazing with gems,
I bear through the world
The Three Flaming Jewels.

With elephant, bull, and lion,
I stepped stately round the capital
Of Asoka's column,
We four beasts bearing between us
The mighty eight-spoked wheel
That through heaven and earth
Rolls irresistibly.

I am the Windhorse!
I am thought at its clearest,
Emotion at its noblest,
Energy at its most abundant.
I am Reverence. I am Friendliness. I am Joy.

Plunging or soaring, I leave behind me
A rainbow track.

from *Song of the Windhorse*
by the Venerable Sangharakshita

13

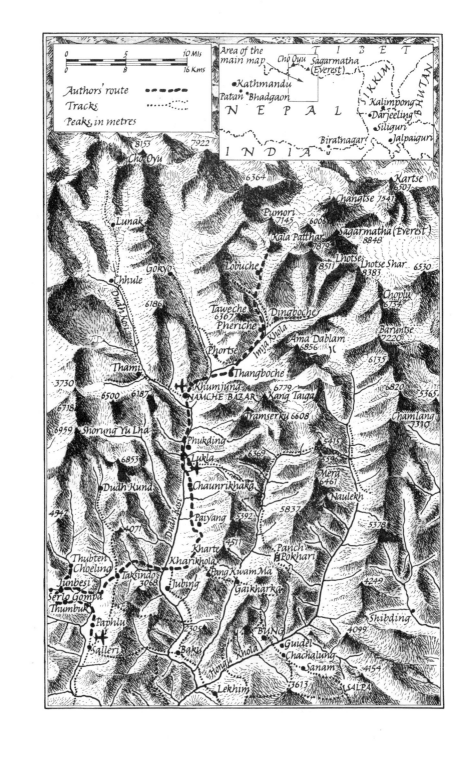

I

Rock-climbing

I leaned out from the ledge, tight against the belay rope, straining my eyes to see why Julie was having difficulty forty feet down the vertical cliff.

'What do I do now?'

'Reach up further with your right hand – there's a really good hold about six inches above you . . .' The wind tore the words from my lips and hurled them into the rocks and heather of the Derbyshire moorland behind me.

'I'm going to fall!'

'Don't worry about it. I've got you.'

I felt the pull as Julie's weight came on the rope, and held her there while she calmed herself and switched hands, putting the left one in the vertical crack she had been following, leaving the other free to reach for a crucial hold on the right. She was moving easily now, feet bridged out either side of the crack, her body gracefully in balance, performing a slow-motion aerial dance upwards against the coarse black rock. It was hard to believe she was new to this sport. Most beginners are rigid, awkward, demanding instructions every step of the way. Julie's demands came infrequently, and I could tell they came from a need not for technical guidance but for reassurance that I was still alert and watching out for her.

A few minutes later she was scrambling onto the ledge beside me, breathless and elated.

'I didn't think I was going to be able to make that move.'

'Hang on, don't sit there. You're still too near the edge. Move over here, behind this boulder.'

'It was just too far for me to reach the first time I tried. I got really scared when I realised I was all tangled up and going to fall. It's funny, there was my rational mind being all cool and sensible about safety-harness and rope and just dangling there when you fall off – and all the time this terrified little voice inside me is saying, "Help! I'm going to crash sixty feet to my death!" And then I just clenched my eyes shut, said "Goodbye world" and let go. And of course nothing happened, so I pulled myself together and climbed it. Did that ever happen to you when you first started?'

'I don't think it ever really stops happening. You're not going to switch off your whole self-preservation instinct just by throwing a bit of safety-harness logic at it. Part of the fascination of climbing is making that instinct work for you and keep you alive, but at the same time controlling it so you don't go rigid with terror and get stuck halfway up a cliff.'

'You mean I've got plenty more of those to look forward to?'

'Isn't that why you do it?'

'Frankly, I'd say no. I like the gymnastics, working out each technical problem like a chess move in my mind and making my body act out the solution – "think high and your body follows." I don't enjoy being scared for its own sake. But in a strange way it does put you very closely in touch with yourself . . .'

Julie coiled the rope as she spoke, while I gathered up the equipment which had been anchoring us to the rockface.

'I think I've learned a lot watching myself react in a tight spot. It comes down to the point where you have to put your trust in the person holding the rope and just go for it. It was the same feeling I had the first time I crossed a busy road with a guide dog. I just had to trust the dog to see what was coming and make the right judgement for me. It isn't as scary now I'm used to it, but my senses are still as sharply tuned as possible, just in case.'

We followed the steep rocky path which wound down to the foot of the crag. Julie's blindness was far more of a disadvantage on this kind of ground than it had been on the rockface. There, she had been able to feel ahead of her with sensitive fingers and create a mental picture for herself as she judged the best way to balance and pull upwards. When walking on rough ground she had to rely on feeling the way my body moved and the signals I gave her through our clasped hands. Even so, she could not be entirely sure whether her foot would come down on top of a stone or at the side of it – until it happened. Then she would have to adjust her balance as best she could.

Bruno was waiting for us at the bottom, yellow tail waving in delight, as if we had been away for a month rather than an hour.

'He's telling you you're daft to go doing dangerous things like climbing up rocks.'

Julie, her arms full of dog, had difficulty replying.

We drove back to London, Julie talking to keep me awake. She enjoys telling a good tale and is always lively and forthcoming in talking about herself. Soon after meeting her, I felt I knew almost every detail of her life. What I had yet to learn was that Julie talked to entertain, not to shock or impress. There were facets of herself I would not discover for many months to come.

She had moved away from her family in Newcastle and settled in London. There she trained as a physiotherapist, a rewarding profession for someone whose visual sensitivity had become channelled through her hands. When her health broke down under the strain of working in a large hospital, she retrained as a telephonist and found a position at a branch of the National Westminster Bank in Victoria. Our climbing excursions were confined to weekends.

At first it had seemed strange to me that someone with such an apparently conventional lifestyle should suddenly develop an interest in an uncomfortable and dangerous sport like climbing. As I learned more about what was involved in coping with everyday life while lacking the benefit of sight, I began to realise that risk and effort were already familiar to Julie in her pursuit of independence.

J ¶ My mother decided to treat me as normally as possible after I lost my sight. I know it was much harder for her emotionally to hold back from interfering, and to watch me stumbling over things or bumping into doors that had been left open, but she realised it was the only way I could learn to cope with everyday living. She told my brothers they must keep their toys off the floor because I couldn't see, and on the whole they were very responsible about it. I think they were quite proud to have a blind sister.

My mother taught me to do the necessary household chores like washing, ironing, cooking and so on. I even learned to knit. I would tell myself I was going to achieve something and wouldn't rest until I'd done it. I was still only eight or nine when I decided to resume running errands to our local shop. As soon as I volunteered to go I was terrified, for I had not been out alone yet. But I felt committed to doing it. I memorised the shopping list and took the money, then set off with a dry mouth and a thumping heart.

I kept to the wall on my left, got past the telegraph pole halfway up the road, then heard two women talking in a doorway and moved out to avoid them. I stopped dead as a car roared round the corner. I felt the wind as it rushed past me. Car noise sounded much louder now I could not see from which direction it was coming. I got to the end of the road as fast as I could. I still had to be careful because cars would park round here and I knew there would be constantly changing obstacles to negotiate just when I was in a desperate hurry to get clear. I had no white stick in those days to warn other people.

I went into the shop as nonchalantly as I could and bought the groceries. Marjie put the things in my bag and said 'Careful with the eggs, mind' as she always did.

Then I made the same cautious journey back home, eggs and all. It was my first foray out into a grey, shimmering world of not-quite-light and not-quite-dark which exists only in sound and touch, and at that time it was very strange and frightening, yet in a way exhilarating. ¶

I felt nervous enough with a sightless adult on the end of a climber's rope. How Julie's mother had coped with the knowledge that her blind eight-year-old was out alone learning to navigate her local streets I would never know, but it was obviously at the root of Julie's ability to pit herself against obstacles and challenges and come out on top.

J ¶ Life opened up dramatically for me once I had Bruno. It was nerve-racking trying to navigate in London traffic with only a white stick, but at the same time I had wild imaginings of being dragged hither and thither by some unruly animal with a mind of its own. I kept putting off making enquiries about a guide dog, and I was twenty-seven before I finally put myself through the interviews and waiting lists and found myself on a one-month residential training course at the Wokingham centre.

When I went to my room on the first night, I sat on the floor for a long time by the empty dog's bed at the foot of my own and wondered how it would feel to go everywhere as the partner of a dog I had never met. I had to train for the first two days with the instructor holding a dog's harness and telling me what I should do and how I should instruct my dog. It was not until I had mastered this that I was able to meet Bruno and begin to practise as a team with him. He had been trained by skilled instructors in the previous six months, and so knew the basic routine perfectly. During our eight years together we have built on this, and now he can guide me to the 'post office', the 'bread shop', the 'station' and many more, just for the asking!

He takes me to work every day on the rush-hour Underground, and is so patient with all the trampling and squashing that goes on. I have quite a lot of the stations memorised, including the back stairways we have to use because dogs are not allowed on the escalators in case they trap their claws. Some stations don't have stairways, so I just have to pick him up and carry him – very uncomfortable for both of us, but he keeps very still. If he did not, I wouldn't be able to lift him at all, as he weighs nearly thirty kilos.

I feel embarrassed if someone gives up a seat for me. After all, I'm as capable as anyone with all their limbs of standing on a moving train. But I try to be polite and look grateful, just because the effort has been made to be friendly. On the whole people are embarrassed and afraid of the disabled, or any sort of handicap. They simply don't know how to react. I try to put people at their ease: if blindness isn't an insurmountable obstacle for me, I don't want it to be for them.

What has always appealed to me about being a switchboard operator is that nobody need ever know I'm blind, and that I can give as comprehensive a service as a sighted operator. I do occasionally get caught out when a customer can't remember the name of the cashier they dealt with and says, 'Oh, you'll know who I mean – she's the only one with long dark hair.' Although I work behind a glass partition which is supposed to cut down the noise, I still have to do battle with the background racket from the word-processor, typewriters, coin-machine, computer terminals, bells, buzzers, the banging of the security doors, and the thudding of the lift. This kind of interference is more disorientating without the stabilising sense of sight to override it. None of us finds the air-conditioning easy to live with, and I'm sure it contributes to my almost daily headaches – although the underlying cause is probably the left-over effects of my original eye condition. ¶

'Isn't there anything you can do to stop the headaches?' I once asked Julie. To me, living with constant headaches seemed almost a bigger problem than being blind.

'Not really. I have tried. It's probably a result of so many operations. As soon as I was examined at birth the doctors noticed that my eyes had a cloudy appearance and diagnosed congenital glaucoma. Yet my family had no history of eye defects.'

'What exactly is congenital glaucoma?'

'It's to do with the internal pressure of the eye. I was born without the channels that drain fluid from the eye. The eye is a very fragile instrument, with a finely balanced fluid level. If this is disturbed in any way, the internal pressure is raised and the various parts of the eye and its nerves can be damaged or destroyed. At eight weeks old I had an operation to construct new drainage channels. It seemed to work at first, but then the pressure started to build up again. My parents were told I would eventually lose my sight, and so I was taught things like braille while I could still see. It seemed like another game at the time. I also learned to play the piano, from braille music, and that helped me to get through the initial depression when I lost my sight.'

'Maybe the headaches are more to do with stress than the operations', I said. 'Plenty of people find cities too hectic to live in for long, even when they can see where they're going. My limit seems to be about three months. Then I have to go and bury myself in a wilderness somewhere, just to catch up on essential commodities like clean air and quiet.'

Anyone meeting Julie for the first time on her home ground could be forgiven for taking some time to realise she cannot see at all. She bustles around an immaculately tidy house (of course it has to be so), makes cups of tea, cooks supper, feeds Bruno and Kerrie, her cat, and keeps a conversation going at the same time.

The first thing one notices in her sitting-room is the collection of china cats of all shapes and colours. The shelves beneath the cats are stuffed with books on adventure and travel. Apart from a few fat packages from the braille library, most of the volumes are in ordinary print. Julie was one of the first to learn how to use an Optacon, which scans print with a camera and converts it to blips for the finger-tips.

'Well, it takes too long for good literature to be transcribed', was Julie's only comment, tea-tray in hand as she closed the door behind her with one foot.

Reading is not Julie's only passion. Her love of music has forced her to overcome her shyness of strangers and go alone (with Bruno) to concerts if no friends are available to accompany her. I began to realise that a guide dog is far more than just a means of transport. It develops a state of mind, an attitude, that comes of being able to make your own decisions and act on them. Julie was emphatic about this.

'Once you've achieved that independence, you *never* want to let it go again, and you fight against all the odds to keep it.'

Julie in her home environment is brisk, smartly dressed, and a lively conversationalist. She takes care to keep up appearances in order to encourage people to offer equality rather than sympathy. As a balance to high-speed city life she meditates and finds the effects so calming that it is worth getting up at 5 a.m. in order to practise for half an hour before doing the housework and setting out on her journey to the bank.

Our conversations tend to roam restlessly from subject to subject and from place to place. The fact that Julie has been unable to travel much does nothing to suppress her lively imagination, her ability to identify vividly with a subject at second hand. For her, visualising a situation from the verbal or printed word is just an extension of what she does every day, working and socialising with people who can see, but having to interpret the world through her other senses.

It was these other senses which had begun to fascinate me during our scrambles out in the hills. I found myself describing the changing scene around us while her mind, hungry for visual information, created inner pictures from my words. Before long, my eyes, looking for the two of us, began to see twice as much as they had before, taking in previously unnoticed detail.

I would hand her leaves, flowers, rocks, and watch her fingers explore the tracery of veins and the ripples of fossilised shells. As she spoke of textures, sounds, smells, I began to enter a world of non-visual perception – a fluid and sometimes elusive world where a person's expression is judged by the rate of breathing and the day's weather by the smell of the wind. I was hooked. Here was a world as fascinating and mysterious as my beloved Himalayas. Aligning my perceptions with Julie's had become as much of a challenge as understanding my extrovert and enigmatic Sherpa friends.

Julie's constant adaptations to the world of sighted people enable her to understand the challenge I enjoy in a lifestyle which involves a lot of travelling, where the prime need is to become adaptable.

To begin with, I travelled in order to climb mountains, regarding the countries visited merely as the location of the next arena for adventure. Success in the world of competitive climbing demands feats of increasing technical skill in ever more exposed situations at progressively higher altitudes. For a while, wholly drawn into this race, I found myself moving from the Alps to the Rockies, and from there to the extreme isolation of frozen Arctic mountains on Baffin Island and in Alaska. The Andes are bigger and even more difficult, so I went there next. Gradually I found myself spending less and less time actually on the mountainside as my eyes began to open to the countries I visited, and to their people. With expedition peaks bagged in Peru and Bolivia and then forgotten, I spent the next eleven months wandering the high Altiplano on my own, learning Spanish, hanging out in windswept villages, or watching the sunrise over the ruins of Machu Picchu and wondering what inspiration had caused its creation.

I first went to the Himalayas to recce for a women's climbing expedition that never happened, and eventually returned from my travels without even looking at the peak I had gone so far to see. I realised I no longer had much in common with expeditions and expeditionaries; instead I was being drawn into the mysteries of the Himalayas themselves. Why was it that the people who lived here had no need to risk their lives in the freezing wastes of ice and snow above their villages? Those I met seemed to radiate a contentment, a sense of completeness, which I found provocative in its very elusiveness.

By the time I went to Tibet with Doug Scott's Shishapangma expedition in 1982, I knew already that my attention was turning elsewhere. After a little climbing I left Base Camp to do what I really wanted – to wander round Tibet alone, although this was prohibited by the Chinese authorities. I doubt if I really appreciated at the time the risks I was taking, for they were, I now see, far more incalculable than those involved in cheating death for the umpteenth time with another test of nerve and physical stamina on one more daunting rockface. And I was not just inviting the inevitable encounters with the bureaucracy of a hostile political set-up – at least, hostile to the extent that I was unwelcome to the Chinese as a lone Englishwoman wandering about freely where I should not have been, among a people who were not overfond of their uninvited political masters. What I suppose I was putting on the line was myself as a person, dependent for my well-being on ordinary people I had never met, in whose language I was scarcely fluent, who risked far more than I did if they fell foul of the authorities for helping me. In short, I was exposing myself to the possibility that love and friendship are more potent than ambition, quick thinking and muscle power. But that is another story.

More recently I worked as a mountain guide on treks in the Nepal Himalayas. As I described my experiences to Julie, her agile mind soon began roaming the mountains too, for she well understood what it meant to put one's trust in others and yet remain free. No matter if photo-fit mental images of yaks and temples were rather approximate at this stage. The imaginative Julie was happy enough; the practical Julie was asking, 'How much would it cost to get there? I wonder how long it will take me to save enough . . . '

2

Go for Everest

It was during my next sojourn in Nepal that I began to take
Julie's wish to travel more seriously. In a respite between
researching a photo-essay and guiding a trekking group
around the Annapurnas, I found myself inside a dark and
smoky Sherpa house and outside rather too much excellent
home-brew. Reflection in the dark often reminds me of Julie
these days. At that moment I could not help thinking, 'She'd
be doing much better than me right now, because her eyes
wouldn't be watering.' Back in Kathmandu, I wrote a letter:

> Julie, there is so much for you here; I meet tourists on the
> trail, their eyes so full of mountains they can't see anything
> else. Up in the hills there are walls of carved 'mani' stones —
> a kind of granite braille in Tibetan script. The temples are
> full of intricate statues in bronze and gold. Here in Kath-
> mandu you pass spice-shops pungent with coriander, cum-
> min, ginger, while next door is an Indian sweet-shop full of
> slowly-evaporated milk candy and sticky jellabees, drip-
> ping with sugar and recycled cooking oil. Just back from the
> sugar-starved hills, the scented atmosphere lures you in,
> and you stuff yourself till you vow you'll never touch the
> things again. (But you do.)

I've told some of my Sherpa friends about you and Bruno. They think I'm kidding. ('Dog school' indeed!) Anyway, they said if you want to come out here, they'll be pleased to lend a hand if you try some trekking.

I wondered how the Optacon would digest Nepalese rice paper and scratchy ball-point.

Three months later, in London, I found Julie reading travel books and making plans to trek in Nepal. She frowned over my proposed route, which meandered sedately through the lower Sherpa villages.

'How much farther is it to Everest Base Camp? Oh, come on, let's go for it – no point doing things by halves.'

Neither of us had any money, so I gave it the treatment I would one of my climbing expeditions and started looking for sponsors. For Julie, a trek would be just as much of a physical and mental challenge.

I was surprised when people told me what a 'kindness' I was showing Julie by 'taking her on holiday'. It hadn't occurred to me to play the role of philanthropist. Besides, I began to wonder who was taking whom. I had not expected her to be much help with expedition preparations, not because she was blind, but because she had no experience of expeditions or of the Himalayas. Within a few weeks she had learned the basic principles involved, and then she threw herself into fund-raising and the accompanying publicity, leaving me free to deal with equipment, food and transport.

'I have to adapt to the sighted world all the time. This is just another adaptation', she observed drily.

If we took Bruno, he would have to stay in quarantine for six months on our return, so Julie made arrangements for him to live with her mother while we were away.

'I wouldn't want him to come to Nepal anyway; there are so many other things he might catch besides rabies. Better he has a six-week holiday.'

Even so, Bruno is so much a part of Julie's life that it was inevitable he would become involved in one way or another, and before long we had become a 'Sponsored Walk in Aid of

Guide Dogs for the Blind'. In addition, Julie had reasons of her own for wanting to make the journey.

'A lot of blind people tend to sit back and have things done for them, largely, I think, because that's what everyone expects. If I show that I can get to Base Camp, then it must be possible for all sorts of other people to do all sorts of other things. Blind people are not helpless or mentally deficient!'

The edge in her voice surprised me.

'Aren't you being a bit over-emphatic? Nobody thinks like that these days.'

'Don't you believe it! There's still a long way to go. A friend of mine was out with her guide dog and she got to a point where she wasn't sure which street they should go down, so she asked a passer-by for directions. And the lady said sure, no problem . . . and then she bent down, lifted the dog's ear and whispered the directions to the dog!'

The conversation collapsed in the ensuing laughter.

'How could she expect it to understand her if she didn't speak Canine?'

During the following few weeks' phone calls, 'Woof!' became the accepted way of introducing ourselves to each other, and I wondered whether we should take ourselves more seriously if we wished sponsors to do the same.

To our great encouragement they did. British Airways gave us tickets, Blacks Alpine donated camping equipment, Adidas promised sweatsuits and boots. Food companies pledged samples of their dried food, and fluffy longjohns arrived in the post from Bingley. Things began to look quite international when two lightweight tents popped out of the Luftpost to join the Swiss Army Knives (which had actually come from Buckinghamshire) – and then, of course, there was The Rope.

The Rope became an acute embarrassment to both of us. A particularly nasty section of the trail up to Namche Bazar prompted me to take a safety rope in case Julie slipped on this narrow and icy stretch, with a steep drop directly below it. This was why I had first taken Julie rock-climbing, to get her used to moving on a rope without getting tangled up in it – a problem common to beginners. As her enthusiasm for the sport had increased, the crags of the Lake District and Derbyshire had found us scrambling up and down for the sheer enjoyment of it. Even so, our journey in the Himalayas was to be a trek – albeit a rugged one – and not a climb in the technical sense. The Press, however, had other ideas. No matter how carefully we explained the facts, reporters would depart with satisfied grins on their faces, half an eye on their notes, and their whole attention on the biggest headline they could muster. The following day we would read such delights as 'BLIND GIRL TO CLIMB EVEREST' or 'PEAK HEROINE'. One report even had Bruno up there on Everest, 'battling the blizzards and glaciers'.

'Perhaps we should ask Blacks to send us some Doggie Crampons.'

'It's not funny! Now I've got to phone the GDBA* and apologise about all the people who'll be ringing them up to tell them Bruno shouldn't be going because of the risk of rabies.'

There were a few more minor panics during our preparations that summer. Julie called me one day almost squeaking with alarm.

'What am I going to do? The BBC wants to come and film me "leading a normal life at home". I don't want millions of people watching how Julie Donnelly washes her socks! How am I going to keep them out of my bedroom? And on top of everything, the reporter's allergic to dogs!'

I suggested she should put a notice saying 'Bruno's grooming room' on her bedroom door. In the event, they filmed us in Derbyshire instead, rock-climbing in the pouring rain.

As summer faded into the gold and russet of autumn, the pace began to slow down. In many ways this was a relief: although we had enjoyed the hectic challenge of organising the trip, it had become increasingly difficult to find the mental 'off' switch, and in the end the strain began to show. Neither of us was sleeping well and we decided we should try to take a

---

*Guide Dogs for the Blind Association.

break from it all before the final preparations. Then I was offered a guiding job in Nepal.

It seemed like the perfect opportunity to make on-the-spot arrangements for local flights, hotel, supplies, and trek staff. My letters so far had elicited only one rather noncommittal reply, and although on my previous visit I had arranged with my friend Ang Dorjee that he would be our *Sirdar**, nothing else was yet confirmed. That was certainly not unusual for the easy-going Nepalese, but we were trying to cram a lot into Julie's six-week leave, and that meant a tight schedule. My departure for Kathmandu also left Julie to cope single-handed with an Expedition Budget that was still in its infancy, not to mention the fact that most of the promised equipment had not actually arrived.

'Oh, don't worry about me, I can cope! November's still a long way off. I'd feel better if I knew everything was fixed up out there. Maybe you can get some discounts, we'll need them! And you look like you could do with a holiday.'

Holiday it most certainly was not. After the longest, stuffiest flight to Kathmandu I can remember, I was totally occupied with my charge of tourists until the second day – which happened to be a Saturday, when everything was closed. Nothing could be done until I returned to Kathmandu at the end of the trek. Then, in a hectic two days, I tried to beat the slow and gentle Nepalese system by flitting round all the appropriate offices and leaving messages for all the 'top people' who, of course, had not come in yet, or had just gone out to lunch, or had just gone home for the day . . . Then I was back in the mountains with another group. This trek, like the first, was anything but restful: treating the various maladies afflicting the clients was varied only by sorting out conflicts and problems among the staff. It was with a feeling of relief that I ushered the group back into their hotel in Kathmandu.

'Telephone, for you.'

I grabbed the phone in one hand while handing out room

---

*Sirdar (Nepali): a guide, co-ordinator of trek staff.

keys with the other, and was greeted with a strong American accent, and a reporter's crisp efficiency.

'Liz Hawley here. I saw a Reuters report about a Julie Donnelly climbing *halfway up Everest* later this year, and quoting an Elaine Brook — which I presume must be you. I suppose Reuters has things slightly wrong and Ms Donnelly will actually be trekking to Base Camp? Is this correct? Can you come round so we can go over the *facts*?'

She probably felt that, as local correspondent, she should get the Reuters record straight.

Liz presides, with tidy efficiency, over a small office at the smart end of the city. She seems to know everything that goes on out there, and I sometimes wonder just how many years she has lived in Kathmandu. Liz doesn't mince words, and in a remarkably short time had our precise schedule noted down. I considered asking her for a copy; it looked much more impressive than my collection of scrawled notes.

'So why Ongdi Trekking rather than the company you usually guide for?'

I explained I had arranged with a friend that he would be our Sirdar and that he was on the permanent staff of Ongdi Trekking.

Liz said, 'I hope you don't mean Ang Dorjee. Because he's dead.'

There was a long silence. I was aware only of a great emptiness. Liz was talking, but her voice seemed to be coming from very far away.

' . . . Everest expedition. I guess he wanted to be the first man to make the summit three times without oxygen . . . ah, I'm sorry, you're upset.'

I just sat there in the little Reuters office, crying, and thinking about Dorjee when he had been so very much alive: Dorjee singing on the trail to Makalu and laughing at the rain and the leeches; Dorjee sorting out a porter strike somewhere in the Annapurnas. He always said he would stick to trekking if it wasn't for the money . . . but maybe Liz was right, maybe he had started to get ambitious. The last time I had seen him he had been packing to fly out to Delhi. Mrs

Gandhi was going to give him a medal for his part in the Indian Expedition's success – his second time to Everest's summit without oxygen. His only comment was, 'I have to go and see these Government people tomorrow. So I had to buy some very expensive new shoes!' He had eyed the package in his hands with mock regret. Surely this throwaway humour did not belong to an ambitious ego?

He was probably the strongest and the best Sherpa on the expedition scene. He knew it, and he no longer had to prove it. Yet in many ways he had become a prisoner of his own success. Ambitious climbers would bid for him, knowing he was the person most likely to get them to the top. And now he was dead.

I walked across the road to the Ongdi Trekking office.

Brian was in a fluster, the lilt of his Indian accent becoming more pronounced in his agitation.

'They won't give us any details about what happened, after they came in here wanting us to change him over from his Makalu expedition . . . look, don't you worry about anything. We'll sort out this trek for you and Julie. I've booked the Paphlu flight you asked for, and I've noted down when you'll arrive in Kathmandu . . . '

I thanked him and retreated. Even thinking about the trek was not something I felt like doing for a while. It was a relief that for the moment things would tick over without me.

There was a letter from Julie waiting for me at the hotel. I curled up in a corner with it, glad to lose myself in someone else's problems.

Hello Little Duck,
I've written so many begging letters that I feel this one won't be complete until I've put something like: 'Please find enclosed a copy of our information sheet'! Expedition funds are now up to £945 and there are still a few places left to try. However, we are going to be living on a very tight budget and I think I've done almost all I can with the jolly old begging bowl! I also had a go at filling out our menu a

bit; I approached Fine Fare and people like that for honey, jam, dried milk, and in one case I even asked for canned meat (thought it might come in useful for the Sherpas). I decided it would be wiser to ask for a variety of things, and then maybe one will come up with something, rather than putting all the metaphorical eggs in one shopping trolley, so to speak. However, there is always a risk of getting eight crates of dried milk, or something equally daft.

I started my vaccinations a couple of weeks ago. My doctor did his nut because I was two weeks late in starting, but I explained how tired I'd been feeling, and all that, and he calmed down. It meant I had to have great doses of cholera and typhoid together, and had a very painful reaction to them, but just about managed to drag myself in to work. This evening I had a polio drop and tetanus, and will have cholera and typhoid boosters next Monday evening, and malaria and gamma globulin a bit nearer the time — which is getting shorter and shorter!

I had a very bad few days in which nothing whatever got done, and I felt physically nauseous just making or seeing a list of things to do with the expedition, but luckily that didn't last, and I'm in great form now — just pretty whacked out by the end of the day.

I've got the ultrasonic mobility aid I think I mentioned to you. So far I have had two lessons with it, and I'm using it on my own between times. It seems that it will be useful in buildings, and to find doorways and outdoor obstacles such as trees, telegraph poles, and other similar landmarks. Not that it can be of any real aid actually on the trail, but I could locate toilet areas, for instance, and buildings in the villages.

Anyway

Anyway — that was the cat's fault, by the way! Must stop now, take care of yourself,

love, Julie

You don't need a sonic aid to locate toilet areas in this part of the world, I thought wryly. All you need is your nose.

1 Julie, aged six, before she lost her sight.

2 Julie today, at home in East London.

3-5 With her yellow labrador guide dog, Bruno, Julie confidently goes shopping and travels on the Underground to the bank where she works the switchboard.

6-7 Elaine solo rock-climbing in Canada (*above*) and at the 19,000-foot summit of Nevada Millachuma in the Bolivian Andes.

8 Supported on a rope held by
Elaine at the top, Julie makes
her first attempt at climbing a
sheer rockface in Derbyshire
before going to Everest.

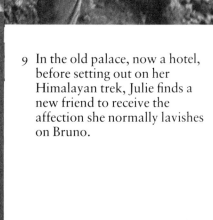

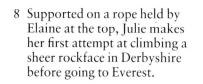

9 In the old palace, now a hotel,
before setting out on her
Himalayan trek, Julie finds a
new friend to receive the
affection she normally lavishes
on Bruno.

I scanned the letter again, wondering if she had been overdoing things. Still, I would be home in a few days.

November London was true to form: rainswept rooftops shining dully and grey shreds of cloud flicking past the windows as the aircraft dropped towards the wet runway. My mind was stupefied from lack of sleep, but still trying to work overtime, running through endless checklists and schedules. My six weeks in Nepal were over. It had not been a happy time, but it had at least been profitable. Everything was booked and confirmed, and our funds and expenses might just meet somewhere in the middle. We were left with four days to pack and get back on the plane.

The next few days seemed to operate on compressed time, like an old film re-run at double speed so that everyone scurries round, to the accompaniment of zippy tunes on the piano. We were scurrying in the flesh, without the benefit of the piano.

Last-minute phone calls to locate equipment which had not arrived at my parents' house in Gloucestershire yielded responses like: 'Oh, it's not been sent yet, luv. You're not going yet are you?'

Mrs Perkins called from the village post office: 'Would you like to come down and collect your chocolate? The delivery lorry got stuck on your hill and he said he didn't fancy having another try . . . ' That hill upset a few of them; the post office smelled of dried onions for an entire week.

Julie's tenth call was about specifications for cine film: 'There are so many numbers involved, and I've never really learned about it, not having the need to use it, so to speak.' I was impressed, not only by the initiative, but by the maintenance of the sense of humour.

A friend called. Three months earlier Peter Hatton had volunteered to collect sponsorship money for the Guide Dog Appeal on our behalves. Now he was volunteering to help manhandle us and our baggage to Heathrow. Brave man.

We collected Julie from the train and started checklisting and packing. The phone rang every ten minutes. The insurance company had decided we were not a good risk and backed out of insuring us. I tried a few others: 'Himalayas, yes. And, ah, by the way, my friend's blind . . . ' After an hour I gave up and went back to the packing. Peter stoically loaded anything that looked full into his car. Mother made cups of tea. And answered the phone. And made more tea. A friend at Julie's bank would arrange insurance.

Peter drove us to London in the rain, with Julie and Bruno wedged in the back between piles of food and equipment. More shopping: tape-recorders, cassettes, extra foam mattresses . . . and a baby-carrier for my friend Samten who was pregnant. Then it all had to be stuffed into kitbags to try to make it look like luggage. One of us would have to wear the baby-carrier.

It was still raining at Heathrow.

'Hello, Tony, sorry we're late!'

'The flight closes in fifteen minutes . . . '

There was a note of disbelief in his voice. It was hard to tell which he was finding incomprehensible, our irresponsible timekeeping or the Giant Red Sausage, alias our kitbag. He had promised us unlimited baggage on behalf of British Airways, and I wondered a little guiltily, as the Giant Blue Sausage was heaved onto the scales, if we had perhaps taken too much advantage of his generosity. There were a lot of lights and cameras, and as I was riffling through connecting flight tickets to get the Giant Sausages checked through to Kathmandu, Julie tried to field questions from three reporters at once. Tony pushed the last of our boxes onto the scales and steered us through security.

'Did you know you had ninety-eight kilos of baggage?' He tried to make it sound casual. He was looking hard at the baby-carrier but decided to say nothing. 'Anyway, I've moved you up to First Class – have a good flight!' He manoeuvred us through the doors, and we collapsed into the pre-packaged comfort of the airline seats.

It felt like a major achievement to have got everything as far as the plane. We toasted our success: 'Getting out of England was the hard part – the Himalayas will be a pushover after this!' I hoped we were right.

34

Sleeping seemed a good idea; it had been in short supply lately, and I would need to be wide awake to get everything through Delhi Airport. As I drifted into unconsciousness, I could hear Julie talking quietly to her tape-recorder, turning away so as not to wake me.

J ¶ I know I should sleep, but somehow I can't just now. Everything has been moving so fast I haven't caught up yet. I try not to think about goodbyes too much before I have to, and then when it comes to it, it's so rushed it almost seems indecent. Bruno and Kerrie have known for days that something was going to happen: when I held them they felt twitchy and apprehensive. I wish I could explain I'll be coming back soon – oh dear, I hope they don't miss me as much as I'm going to miss them . . . ¶

But even the irrepressible Julie could not stay awake for long. Some hours later she continued her monologue into that unresponsive machine.

J ¶ Hello again tape-recorder. I'm going to be more cheerful this time! After a sleep and breakfast, Elaine prodded me and indicated that we were to visit the flight deck to meet the Captain and crew. I sat down in front of the bank of controls feeling quite at home fingering all those buttons and knobs which remind me of a multi-position switch-board. Captain Green held my hand against the lever as he altered the aircraft's altitude, and I was surprised at the ease and sensitivity of the controls. For the only time on the flight (except for take-off and landing) I had a powerful sense of aerial movement. That was most exhilarating; but how noisy it is in there! We are flying the new fast route over Russia, and will soon be in Delhi. ¶

3

Kathmandu

The transit system at Delhi Airport has to be seen to be believed. After elbowing your way on and off the service bus through a night of tropical heat and diesel fumes, you queue-jump the milling crowd at immigration and duck through into 'baggage claim'. A security officer takes away your passport to ensure you don't make a sudden mad dash for freedom into India without a visa. Then you collect your luggage (all ninety-eight kilos of it) and trolley it back to where you have just come from. In my case, it took two trolley journeys plus a side trip to track down the officer with my passport.

Julie was getting anxious. 'There's less than an hour to our connecting flight!' I had a faint suspicion we were not going to make it, but it was worth a try. We had to trolley our gear out onto the tarmac and wheel it down to the other terminal, half a kilometre away. There was such a noise out there that Julie's sense of direction became totally confused, and she kept veering off towards the runway and having to be retrieved. The trolleys were so battered that staying close together meant we were constantly crashing into each other. It took a while to reach our destination, only to find that the architects had forgotten to include a ramp for the trolleys, which had to be lifted up a large step.

'Esther Rantzen would have a field day out here,' I muttered as I pitted my forty-five kilos against a fifty-kilo trolley.

A man with a clipboard was patrolling the transit lounge. I thrust our tickets at him.

'I am sorry, the flight is full.'

'But this sticker means we have a confirmed reservation on it.'

'That is true. But the flight is already full.'

No argument could prevail against that kind of logic. We sat down in the black plastic chairs and watched the lounge empty as the passengers boarded the Kathmandu flight. Our flight. This sort of thing is not unusual in India, which was why I had also made reservations on the afternoon flight, but we were now faced with a rather dreary seven-hour wait. Julie found the lack of reliability hard to accept.

'How different from Heathrow and British Airways. It's hard to believe a system can change so much at the end of a journey. I thought if you checked baggage through you didn't have to collect it till you reached the final destination.'

'No automation out here,' I said, as jauntily as I could. 'But our BA baggage allowance doesn't extend to other airlines, and at least transit baggage isn't normally weighed again.'

'Aren't they going to *notice* that lot can't possibly be forty kilos?'

'Yes, well, that's why I didn't want it sitting around an empty transit lounge all day.'

'Is this going to be expensive?'

'Could be.'

'I find it very unnerving when travel arrangements are unreliable. I can make journeys with Bruno on unfamiliar routes but I have to plan every transfer meticulously. If anything goes wrong it's very hard to extricate myself without making things worse – rather like being in a quicksand where you don't dare move. There's no guarantee there will be a convenient passer-by to tell you where you are and advise on what to do next – or even if you're going to be stuck in wherever-it-is for the night! I know you're here to navigate now, but the uneasy feeling is still there underneath . . .'

37

When I saw how worried she looked I began to wish I had not mentioned the problem. We tried to assuage our fears of a devastated budget by packing all the heavy things into the hand luggage. The baby-carrier was now stuffed with film canisters and packets of powdered pineapple drink. I could tell Julie's tension was increasing with her awareness of every potential problem.

'I wouldn't have minded if I'd been expecting the delay. But that, and having to worry about the excess baggage, spoils everything somehow.'

Unexpected delays and problems are an integral part of expedition travel in Asia. I hoped Julie had not built up too many preconceived ideas about this journey and so would be disappointed in the real thing.

The man with the clipboard reappeared, and I tried gently to make him feel guilty for pushing us off the earlier flight as he made his way inexorably towards the Giant Sausages.

'How much luggage do you have here?'

'Oh, I'm not sure, ah . . . it's not as heavy as it looks.'

The baggage handler was right on cue; picking up a large black duffle from the top of the pile, he waved it around in one hand.

'This isn't even four kilos!'

It pays to keep a duffle of foam mattresses accessible for these occasions. No one was really convinced, but honour had been preserved, we had waited all day, and the flight was almost empty. They could afford to be generous, and our embarrassing luggage was waved through.

We flew eastwards along the line of the Himalayas for an hour. I tried to describe the distant mountains to Julie, but we were both too tired to find much enthusiasm for them. Several flights must have landed in quick succession, because Kathmandu Airport was jammed with people milling around looking for baggage, exchange, and visa forms.

'Thank goodness you're here. I was wondering what had happened to you!' Brian extricated himself from the crowd, looking a little ruffled. 'Here, give me your passports, I know someone who can get it all through quickly.'

He vanished again into the mêlée while I found a quiet corner in which to leave Julie guarding our desperately heavy hand-luggage. Then I joined Brian in the free-for-all at the baggage counter in search of the rest of it. He was fuming at the devious behaviour of the porters.

'Always the same, never there when you want them. Just dump it on the tarmac and disappear, then they'll show up at the last minute, carry it a few yards and plague you for baksheesh. Which ones are yours? My God, what have you *got* in here?'

Brian had a rich, musical voice which brought out the humour he found in both the chaotic system and his annoyance with it. I found his complaints delightfully entertaining, and sure enough, after the initial manhandling, a squad of porters descended on the bags and whisked them through to Customs. He managed to fend off their most outrageous demands for baksheesh while simultaneously convincing Customs that it was quite normal for two lady trekkers to have this amount of luggage. Then he chivvied the porters and bags out to the waiting car.

We stepped out into a city of dusty red sunset and silhouetted pagodas. There was too much bustle to describe the scene to Julie, but I could tell she was taking in her own impressions.

J ¶ It was so nice to be in the cool evening air and away from the jostling stuffiness of the airport. Someone stepped forward and hung a katak – a 'good-luck' silk scarf – around my neck. It was Jangbu, our Sherpa cook, welcoming us to Nepal. I could tell he was small by the direction of his voice. He sounded very young, and jolly, and although his English was limited I felt he was going to be good company.

We squeezed into the back of the car and drove through the city. The first thing I noticed about Kathmandu was the quantity and noise of the traffic, the bewildering variety of horns, hooters and bells creating an atmosphere of frenetic speed and impatience. It took a while to get used to it, and to realise that in the crowded centre of the town it was, in fact, quite slow-moving. ¶

Brian was still muttering about the airlines. 'They're getting worse, I'm sure they are – always overbooking . . . I drive out to meet confirmed passengers not knowing if they're going to show up or not – your names were on the passenger list for this morning and I spent an hour looking for you. How are you going to get your food shopping done now you're so late? I've got to get Jangbu and the supplies on the six o'clock bus to Jiri tomorrow morning or he won't be able to meet you in Paphlu . . . '

'We can do the shopping tomorrow and he can leave the day after. We can wait for him somewhere.'

Brian's eyebrows registered surprise and relief, as well as amusement. He was obviously used to dealing with tourists who squawked loudly at the first sign of an upset schedule. From our point of view, a day of waiting up in the mountains would be quite pleasant. Usually the cook would simply have done the shopping himself, but Brian had arranged this excursion at my request, so that we could choose our own food – and so that Julie could explore the market.

We reached the hotel and piled out of the car like a circus act where things keep coming, and coming . . . a bevy of bellboys pounced on the Giant Sausages, bags and boxes, and disappeared upstairs with them, leaving a trail of powdered pineapple juice on the deep pile carpet.

Brian shook his head. 'What *have* you got in there? Oh well, never mind, we'll talk about it tomorrow. Give me your passports again, and I'll arrange your trekking permits.'

Julie said, 'I forgot my passport photos.'

'Never mind. I can fix it. I'll send Jangbu over tomorrow morning to take you shopping.' He retreated to the car before we could inflict any more problems on him.

The receptionist handed me the key and a letter; while Julie made a dive for the bathtub, I flopped on the bed to read.

Dear Elaine,

I am sorry I cannot meet you in Kathmandu after all. I have to go back to my village. But I will come and meet you in Paphlu. I hope you will have a good journey.

your friend,
Tapkhay Lama

Tapkhay, a Sherpa monk, was establishing a new monastery and school in his village near Paphlu. In the past I had helped him with his fund-raising, and he had invited Julie and me to visit his village. I had written to tell him when we would be coming, but without much hope of the letter reaching him in this land of haphazard communications. Then, quite by chance, we had run into each other in front of the King's palace just before I left Kathmandu – was it only six days ago? He would be going back home soon, he said, and would meet us either here or in Paphlu.

Julie emerged from a steaming bathroom and tripped over the baby-carrier, jolting me out of my reminiscences to clear a gangway through our piles of baggage.

'I've run the bath again for you. What did the letter say?'

'Tapkhay's meeting us in Paphlu. Should you be running around in your skin? You'll catch a cold, or double pneumonia or something.'

'No I won't. You get colds from germs, not from being cold. Anyway, I'm warm.'

I let the hot water soak away the airport grime and tension, and remembered how tired I was. Too tired to sort out the bags, or the budget, or any of the other chores clamouring for attention.

Jangbu waited patiently in reception while we drank cups of tea and tried to wake up.

'Maybe we go to i-store first?'

I smiled as I remembered the Nepalese pronunciation of an initial 's' before a consonant. The 'i-store' was a large building in the grounds of Colonel Ongdi's house, and a long taxi ride to the outskirts of Kathmandu. It was worth the journey, as I was able to remove all the manufactured food Jangbu had already packed and replace it with the dried food we had brought from England. We explained to him that we were vegetarians, but that he could buy meat for the Sherpas along the way if he wanted to. He nodded philosophically and gathered up the cans and jars to replace them somewhere in the depths of the store.

Outside in the sun some Sherpas were pitching tents and washing them down, while others were sponging blue camping mattresses and hanging them out to dry on a length of old climbing rope. A white Mercedes with Bhutanese plates was parked in the driveway; the Colonel was just leaving for the office.

The last time I had seen Mrs Ongdi she had been resplendent in silk and diamonds; today she was wearing her Wednesday dress and slippers, with a cheerful and homely manner to match.

'Hello, how nice to see you. Would you like a cup of tea?' She turned to Jangbu. 'Come along, we must make some tea. She lapsed into Nepali for Jangbu's benefit, and he went into the house.

Julie was admiring the flowers; the elegant brick house with its pillars and archways was covered with a climbing honeysuckle, heavy with orange flowers.

'It's so lovely to sit in warm sunshine with flowers everywhere, and in late November! Orange is my favourite colour.' Her fingers explored the waxy petals and twisting, vine-like stems.

Mrs Ongdi smiled and picked one for her. 'I like this one because it is one of the few that blooms in the winter. There are so many in the summer.'

It was hard to imagine greater profusion of colour. Many of the exotic plants found in English gardens originated in Asia, and are bigger and brighter in their homeland.

Jangbu brought the tea, and spread cushions on the lawn beside the rose garden. Even here there was a row of pitched tents.

'You must find it very busy with your work coming home with you every day like this?'

'Yes, of course it is, but what to do? If you don't have your equipment right under your nose, it's inevitable that you will get . . . leakage, you know.' What an appropriately gentle euphemism.

Julie had been stroking the Ongdis' pet Alsatian while we were talking. Now, it suddenly growled, snapped at her hand, and slunk back into the house. I must have looked far more alarmed than Julie, because Mrs Ongdi was quick with her reassurance.

'Don't worry, he's had all his shots, and he's not dangerous – he just gets a bit irritable sometimes, that's all.'

I knew Julie would find it hard to overcome her love of animals and refrain from stroking and cuddling the dogs we would meet. She had come straight from England, and had never had any bad experiences with dogs. I had felt the same until I had been mauled and gone through the resulting series of rabies shots. For this trip, I knew the fear I had learned would have to do for both of us.

Jangbu reappeared with Dawa the cookboy.

'Shopping?'

Dawa was a head taller and two shoulders broader than our cook. He shuffled his scuffed shoes in the dirt, a little shy of us at first, then gave us a lopsided grin and shambled along behind us like an overgrown bear-cub. We followed the narrow lane down towards the main road. There was little traffic here apart from a few bicycles, usually with extra passengers balanced precariously on the crossbar. One man had loaded his bike with two enormous baskets of 'suntalas' (tangerines) and was wheeling it carefully between the potholes. On either side of the lane were the large new luxury houses of Kathmandu's élite, brick-built and architect-designed, but still unmistakably Nepalese with their balconies, pagoda roofs and arched colonnades overgrown with vines. Interspersed with these were the original brick-and-ceramic tile houses of the Newari farmers out in the valley.

At the main road Jangbu hailed a taxi which took us through the outskirts of Kathmandu. Here Hindu temples appear against modern Government buildings, and sleek new minibuses full of plump tourists swerve round barefoot porters carrying sacks of rice on a *namlo** across their foreheads. We scrambled out in Thamel, at the edge of the old part of the city, a narrow street bordered by tall balconied tenements, like those of medieval England. What a contrast to the quiet suburbs we had just left! People, bicycles and rickshaws all jostled for precedence with large and obstructive sacred cows, hopping out of the way of taxis nosing through where taxis really did not belong. The general din of people and traffic was punctuated by the occasional extra-loud bleep of a horn – usually from right behind us – which would make Julie jump, as if she had received an electric shock. Stepping round sacred cow dung, we decided this was no place for a blind person to travel comfortably on foot. I hailed a passing rickshaw and began a heavy bargaining session, Jangbu and Dawa grinning with delight at my English-accented Nepali and elaborate show of righteous indignation.

'How much to Asan Tole?'

'Fifty rupees.'

'Fifty is a joke! I'll pay two.'

'Twenty, or I'm not going.'

'Why should I pay you twenty, when I can take a taxi for five?'

'All right, five then.'

'A taxi is more comfortable, I'll only pay three.'

'Okay! Because you are my friend and speak Nepali, and because your friend is blind, I will take you for four rupees.'

I paused for a moment, wondering how Julie was going to climb aboard a contraption she had never seen, but the driver helpfully dismounted and held the thing still while she ran her hands over the bicycle frame, the double seat and footrest at the rear, and the little step by the back wheel. Then she scrambled up as if she had been doing it all her life. The folding

---

**namlo* (Nepali): a woven carrying-strap.

canopy over the passenger seat was pushed back (or more likely had collapsed) giving an all-round view of the narrow streets with their tall, gabled houses. Above us, women in bright saris watched the bustle in the street from carved wooden balconies and windows, while on either side little hole-in-the-wall shops displayed their wares about the doorways in a blaze of colourful clothes, rugs, pictures and second-hand trekking equipment. I soon found it was unnecessary to describe the passing scenery to Julie; she was in the first throes of what was obviously going to be a lifelong addiction to rickshaw rides.

J ¶ Rickshaws are an ideal way to get the feel of a place. No wonder some tourists actually pay the outrageous fifty rupees when they first arrive and haven't got used to the local money. The pace of a rickshaw is slow, so there's time to take in what is going on around as you clatter by. I could tell when we were passing side-roads because the wind changes when the building line drops away. I could hear the tradespeople at work, passers-by talking and laughing, flute-sellers demonstrating their instruments. And there were the smells from hundreds of little shops and stalls in the market area – spices, fish and meat (raw and cooking), vegetables, the pungent tang of leather, the subtle smells of herbs mixed with oil and acrid woodsmoke – the list is endless, and the overall effect is unforgettably Kathmandu.

Driving along in a car is a comparatively boring experience for a blind person, as the windows shut out all the sounds and smells – the equivalent of driving along with all the windows blacked out. Another gasp from Elaine interrupted my sightseeing.

'What's up?'

'I think there may be a definite advantage in *not* being able to see what we almost collide with every couple of minutes.'

I could tell our progress was fairly erratic, but as it was beyond my control it was easy not to feel too concerned about it. All too soon we reached the vegetable market and dismounted. Jangbu and Dawa had not managed to find themselves a rickshaw, but nevertheless had arrived at the same time as us. ¶

Jangbu's first purchase was a *doko* – a large, conical carrying-basket woven from strips of split bamboo. This he handed to Dawa, who hefted it onto his broad shoulders and lumbered along behind us, dropping the vegetables we bought into the basket. It was a complicated business: I would consult Jangbu as to whether an item was currently available along our trekking route (in which case we would not buy it here), then translate into English for Julie and make sure she liked to eat it. Some of the vegetables were familiar – cauliflowers, tomatoes and onions looking much the same as they do anywhere. Others defied translation. A bundle of bright pink carrots lay beside bunches of giant white radishes and some greenish-brown spiky things which I could only hand to Julie and confess I had never tried.

'Perhaps we won't bother with these then.' Her hands explored the contents of the next basket. 'What are these?'

'A sort of miniature white aubergine with mauve stripes.'

'And these?'

'Fresh green chillies. Red-hot.'

'No thanks!'

Jangbu interrupted. 'Oh no, the green ones aren't hot – it's the red ones that are hot.'

'I've tried the green ones and they're quite enough for me. If you're taking any red ones, save them for the Sherpas.'

Jangbu and Dawa chuckled at the weakness of English palates.

We moved to the spice-shops, and I struggled to remember the Nepali names for everything. We were on safe ground with root ginger, peppercorns, cummin and fennel, but the scoopfuls of anonymous-looking ready-ground powders were mystery packages as far as I was concerned. Still, our cook seemed cheerfully confident that he had everything under control, and for the moment I was content to follow his lead.

We continued to pick our way between piles of scrubbed vegetables and bamboo baskets. Julie was interested in everything.

'Ooh, what's this?'

'Dried sprats.'

'Ugh.'

Jangbu was buying rice.

'Hang on a minute, Jangbu – can't we get rice up in the villages?'

'Yes, we can – but not proper tourist rice. Village rice is only good enough for Sherpa food.'

'We'd rather eat Sherpa-food rice if that's all right with you. This Kathmandu white rice is like plastic.'

'What's happening?' asked Julie.

'Polished or brown rice?'

'Brown, most definitely. Oh, I see, of course, they think we think white is better.'

Our cook was shaking his head resignedly and returning the rice to the shopkeeper. Then, with an effort, he regained control of the situation.

'We should go and pack this food now. I'll come to the hotel and collect the equipment you can't take on the plane.'

He hailed another rickshaw and we departed for a belated lunch. Narayani's, my usual haunt, is a redecorated single room at the edge of Thamel, with a glass shelf of apple pies at one end and a hissing espresso machine at the other, wobbly wood-and-plastic tables squeezing in between. It is noisy and crowded, and the waiters are half-asleep, but it is also cheap and clean, and the food is excellent.

'Hello, Mr Narayani! When are you going to build your extension so we can find somewhere to sit?'

'Oh, you know, sometime . . . sometime! Come over here, I can find you somewhere . . . '

He ushered us to a table already occupied by two bearded Americans. Sociable place, Narayani's. It was clear that the Americans had returned from a long spell in the hills, for they ordered two main courses each. One of them had just completed a term in the Peace Corps (the American volunteer

47

service) and was talking about his impressions between mouthfuls of buffalo steak.

'I've been working on a development project in a village near Charikot, about a day from the new road. Hindu village – Chettris and Brahmins – the other tribes that call themselves Hindus aren't proper Hindus and the Chettris and Brahmins don't accept them as such.'

I was interested to learn more about the Hindu villages.

'Well, I sure had the opportunity to learn about them, I was invited into so many homes. They think you're real special if you work for the Peace Corps . . . but I guess I'm not really interested in their past. I'm interested in what they're doing now, where they're going. They need more industry, more roads, more development . . .'

I wasn't so sure, but said nothing. After they had left, even Julie was a bit subdued.

'Are there a lot of aid projects here?'

'Everyone is in here: British, New Zealanders, Americans, Russians, Chinese – even Indians. Most of what they do is really useful, but it's not very helpful if it creates a demand for timber, because tree-planting isn't keeping up with the deforestation as it is. There's a very sad joke in Nepal about an island growing in the Bay of Bengal which should be Nepalese territory because it's made of Nepalese topsoil that's been washed away. Once the trees are stripped off, the monsoon erodes the soil very quickly.'

We still had to pack; Jangbu would be coming round in less than an hour. Back in the hotel, we surveyed the mountain of gear despondently.

'Ten kilos each isn't much to go camping with, is it?'

'We'll be meeting Jangbu with the rest of it after three days. So we wear all our clothes, and just pack what we can.'

We borrowed a spring balance from reception (they must have had guests with this problem before) and carefully weighed out two small kitbags containing tents, sleeping-bags, mattresses and so on. The rest lay in a heap on the floor. Jangbu arrived.

'Oh. Not quite ready?'

'Nearly! Look. This lot . . .', pushing boots and jackets to one side of the room, 'is warm clothes and boots for three Sherpas. By the way, what size does our Sirdar take? We won't see him till he meets us in Paphlu, but I have to give you his things tonight.'

'Oh, he's *fat*. Much bigger than me, but not quite as big as Dawa.'

'What was that?' asked Julie.

'We've got a fat Sirdar. Hope the stuff fits.'

Jangbu was being helpful. 'Is this what I take on the bus?'

'Not all of it!' I retrieved the baby-carrier. 'Some of it is presents for friends and some ours to leave in Kathmandu.'

I pushed a heap to the other side of the room. 'This is all you need to take.'

Even so, by the time we had stuffed it into a kitbag, it dwarfed the diminutive Jangbu as he hoisted it on his back.

'If we take extra porters and give them i-small loads, we can get from Jiri to Junbesi in three days. Have a good flight, see you in Junbesi!'

The Giant Red Sausage pattered off down the carpeted corridor on Jangbu legs.

We slept.

We were left with one day in Kathmandu in which (due to having spent a day in Delhi Airport) to complete two days' chores. Julie decided to sit this one out, in the hotel garden, with her tape-recorder. I headed for the office to make final arrangements with Brian and the Colonel. Then I hurried three doors down to the Tiger Tops office.

Lisa Van Gruisen is one of the few people in Kathmandu to bother with Western fashions. Her private office is furnished with Tibetan rugs, a mahogany desk covered with papers, and a photograph of herself walking down Thamel with Robert Redford. She stood up, towering over me, and wrung my hand. Her attitude wasn't 'British Raj', but her accent certainly was.

'I'm so glad you could come in before I left – I'm supposed to be flying to India this afternoon. Look – we've decided to invite you and Julie down to our Jungle Lodge as a Christmas present . . . but can you go through the details with my secretary, because I really *do* have to rush . . . '

I sat by the typewriter and went through dates and flight reservations while Lisa shuffled papers into a briefcase and made a dash for the door.

'Bye – see you when we're both back in Kathmandu.'

'Have a good flight. I'm still jealous of that photograph!'

I could hear her laughter receding down the corridor.

I was late back to the hotel.

'I've been so hungry and bored waiting for you.'

Julie's frustration dissipated over lunch, to my relief, but the situation left me uneasy. Without me, Julie was going to be completely stranded, unable to move around, and to a certain extent isolated from other people by the language. Yet there would always be times when I would have to go off to attend to something and leave her on her own. I knew she was too sensible to do anything dangerous, but how hard was it going to be for her emotionally? In England she was active and independent because she had a system which enabled her to be so. I began to realise how much courage it had taken to leave these props behind.

Julie opted to come with me for the afternoon. First stop was Shona's Trekking Shop. We squeezed between the down jackets, rucksacks and rain-trousers festooned around the doorway, and I peered into the dark interior, looking for Shona.

'Hey, there you are at last! Come in and I'll get you some tea.'

She was young and pretty, hardly a trace of Tibetan accent left in her flawless English. Three small children romped round the Gaz stoves and rows of boots.

'Here's the camping mattresses you wanted, and we need sunglasses and nylon string.'

Shona rummaged around the dusty shelves and pulled out a coil of blue avalanche cord.

'What d'ye need nylon string for?'

Lindsay's Scottish accent was unmistakable, as was the six-foot bulk which moved out of the shadows at the back of the shop.

'Hello Lindsay, how are you?'

'Terrible.' He attempted a grin but I could see he meant it. 'I'm trying to find a tent I can afford to buy.'

'I thought you were climbing Kanguru?'

'Couldn't afford the fees. So I'm going trekking.'

'That's nothing to feel terrible about.'

'The trekking's supposed to make me feel better. I just had a bad season guiding, that's all. The Sirdar was useless at everything except lining his own pockets, and the cook couldn't cook. So there I was with a very cheesed-off bunch of trekkers, and finished up having to run the whole thing myself, organise the porters, do the cooking, the lot.'

My last season had been marred by one individual more interested in his business sidelines than doing a good job as Sirdar, and Lindsay and I were soon involved in a mutual complaining session. I had always so much enjoyed working with Sherpas in the mountains, it had been a disappointment to find one interested only in profits.

' . . . So there we were at ten thousand feet, in the rain, and he'd overloaded the porters so much that half of them didn't get in with the tents.'

Julie was laughing at all this indignation. 'Surely they're not all as bad as that?'

'Only a very few, but then people complain and it makes it bad for the others.'

'Don't start worrying – it wasn't Ongdi staff.'

Lindsay resumed his pursuit of an affordable tent, while we finished the chores and took a rickshaw back to the hotel. The manager had promised to take us on a tour of the buildings which had been converted from an old Rana palace.

At first there were a few non-sequiturs: we wanted to hear about the decadent deeds of the Ranas, while he, of course, wanted to tell us about his fine hotel.

'Tell us how the Ranas lived.'

'The Ranas built many palaces. We converted this one into the Shanker hotel in 1964; it has one hundred rooms . . . '

The elaborate woodcarvings and plaster mouldings were especially interesting for Julie, and while her fingers got busy on the decorations, her questions probed the history of the palace.

'Why are there fleurs-de-lis mixed in with these flowers in the plasterwork on the pillars?'

'Because the Rana Maharaja who built the palace at the turn of the century employed a French architect.'

'Who were the Ranas?'

'They were prime ministers. I have to go back into history here. Originally, Nepal was many small kingdoms; even in the Kathmandu Valley there were three kingdoms – Patan, Bhaktapur, and Kathmandu. The kings were always fighting each other. Even when one king succeeded in conquering the others and uniting Nepal, the power of the king lasted only three generations. As the Ranas grew more powerful, the king became no more than a figurehead. And of course the Ranas became very rich, and the different families began to compete with each other, each trying to build a more wonderful and elaborate palace than the other. They had their family in here, as well as thousands of serving girls, and their word was law. They could have anything they wanted, just by speaking – there was no constitution. Then, when there was a revolution here in 1951, many Ranas ran away to India, and their palaces became converted into offices and so forth. We rented this one at first, then we bought it. It's so big – we have dining-rooms, ballrooms, guest rooms – but we're still using only a quarter of the original palace.'

Back in our room, Julie got into the spirit of the thing, stretching out on the brocade couch beside the carved archway of the window.

'Mm . . . wonder what it felt like to be a Rana princess with hundreds of servants and anything you want, just for the asking . . . '

'Come on, your Majesty, we've got to pack.'

'Pooh, I bet Ranas didn't have to hassle around worrying about going over their ten kilos baggage allowance.'

Most likely they did not, but we did, and were having to perfect the art of creating heavy but inconspicuous hand luggage. All our clothes were set in a pile ready for a hurried start at 5 a.m. Then we made an almost successful effort to catch up with the expedition accounts. After a postcard-writing session (alternating one for me, one for Julie) it was hardly worth sleeping for the two hours that remained before it was time to get up again.

4

Tapkhay Lama

Julie found time afterwards to tape her impressions of the journey.

J ¶ At 5.30 the grand dress-up began – from thermal under-wear and long climbing socks outwards, many layers of shirts and jumpers, various things wound around our persons, ending up eventually with down jackets, gaiters, and heavy boots. With so much on, I couldn't bend over far enough to fasten my own gaiters! Elaine tipped me over, horse-shoeing style, and fastened them for me, winding a few extra pairs of socks around inside them for good measure. Then we decked ourselves with cameras, tape-recorders and so on, and moved ourselves and our lug-gage – awkwardly – downstairs.

For me, the car journey merged into the time waiting for our bags to be checked at the airport. I took my weekly malaria pill that morning, finally realised they violently disagreed with me, and had to concentrate hard on trying not to faint. Brian interrupted my misery by taking my arm.

'Let me guide Julie – she's my pass for coming with you into the departure lounge.'

We shuffled through Security, where the ladies prodded our bulkiness a couple of times.

'Trekking?'

They'd seen it all before. We shuffled over to the seats to wait. Elaine was starting to worry.

'Are you going to be okay on the flight?'

'Oh yes, I'm feeling better already, I think.'

Brian waited with us in case the flight was cancelled because of the morning fog, but it cleared after an hour and we walked out onto the tarmac. Then it was a case of one foot on the step, the other on the wheel, and hauling yourself in. I'd never been in such a small plane – only five passengers – and I was surprised at how noisy and rattly it was. From time to time Elaine would yell above the bedlam to let me know what we were flying over.

'There's the new road to Jiri – Jangbu and crew will be well on their way by now . . . oh, that's nice, the pilot's just swung round towards the mountains a bit so we can take photos.'

There was a long interlude of scuffling and clicking shutters, then more shouting close to my ear.

'We're just flying over the Lamijura Pass – eleven and a half thousand feet – and we're only about a hundred feet above it . . . my goodness, there's a gompa just gone past the left-hand window!' (She explained afterwards that the *gompa** was built halfway up a large cliff.) Then, with a lot of rattling and bumping, we landed on the dirt runway at Paphlu. ¶

Scrambling out of the plane, I scanned the small crowd of people waiting at the airstrip. A familiar red-robed figure walked towards us and draped kataks round our necks.

'Welcome to Paphlu! *Namaste* Elaine. Hello Julie, I am Tapkhay Lama!'

Suddenly, with Tapkhay's boisterous energy and good humour, the desolate airstrip seemed a much friendlier place, and despite the tiredness we laughed and congratulated each other on having met up again in this land of huge distances and little transport. Tapkhay had left his village

---

**gompa* (Tibetan): place for meditation (temple/monastery).

before dawn to be sure of arriving here in time.

'Excuse me, are you with Ongdi Trekking? I am Lhakpa. Your Sirdar.'

I stared at him. He was about the same height as me, and very slim. I almost said, 'You can't be, our Sirdar's fat!' – then realised he wouldn't know what I was talking about. I shook his hand, introduced everyone, and suggested a cup of tea – my favourite solution in times of decision, or any other time come to that. We scrambled up the dusty bank to a little wooden-plank 'hotel'. Lhakpa ordered some tea, while Julie and I made a dive for the back room where we thankfully stripped off our layers and layers of clothes. We emerged looking much thinner, and the two Sherpinis who had just appeared with our luggage burst into fits of giggles.

'These Sherpinis are coming with us,' explained Lhakpa.

I had asked Brian if he could arrange female porters for us, as I thought they would be moral support for Julie if I had to leave her for a while. Some of the Khumbu Sherpinis work as porters every November and December when there is a slack period on the farms. These two looked too sleek and smartly-dressed for farm girls, but I thought no more of it and headed for the tea.

'So you are coming to Thumbuk today?' Tapkhay's enthusiasm to show off his village and his new gompa was bubbling over.

'We'll see how far we get today; I don't suppose we walk as fast as you do. We have to meet the cook in Junbesi the day after tomorrow, in the evening.'

I could see Lhakpa looking puzzled by this last remark, because he had not been told where we would be meeting Jangbu, and Thumbuk and Junbesi lay in completely the opposite direction from the Everest route. I figured we had a month – plenty of time for a small detour, and it would all be good acclimatisation. I could see Lhakpa privately resigning himself to the eccentricities of foreign tourists.

Although he still looked fairly young, Lhakpa gave the impression of having worked with Westerners for some time. His clothes were smart by Solu-Khumbu standards, and I noticed that he addressed Julie and me by our first names as soon as we were introduced. This is our custom, not theirs. Sherpas and Nepalis will address each other as *sati* ('friend') or *diddi* ('sister') and so on.

Tapkhay's energy soon had us all on the road, with his nephew carrying the doko full of camping gear. The trails around these larger, more well-to-do villages are better than the ones further up in the mountains, but even so they are quite steep and rocky in places. Julie and I were having to concentrate hard on navigating. It was necessary to refine our hand-communications to accommodate conditions we had not come across in England. We had never worked out a formal system of signals: it was something that had built up instinctively between us on our scrambles together. Here I was resorting to verbal directions far more than usual, and until we could internalise the new conditions, these would have to do.

One of the most difficult obstacles, oddly enough, was the single-file rut in the path, worn by the passing of human and bovine feet. In order to keep her balance as stable as possible, Julie tends to splay her feet as she walks, so these narrow ruts would trip her every time. The only solution was for me to call 'ditch' every time I saw one coming up; if I forgot the warning I would immediately have Julie tripping up and falling against my back. The other disadvantage of having to walk in tight single file was that my rucksack got in Julie's way as she followed close behind me. In the end Lhakpa gave it to one of the Sherpinis, and this made the narrow sections much easier.

In places, the path was wide and level, giving us a respite from navigating and a chance to enjoy the surroundings. Above us, Chiwong gompa perched on its cliff. Already I found it hard to remember that we had flown past it only this morning . . . that we had been away from the city less than a day. The noise of the traffic and the crowds had never belonged out here; only the wind in the pine forest and the splashing of a clear green river at the bottom of the hill. Air travel transplants your body more quickly than your mind can catch up. For the next few days we felt we were living in a dreamworld where anything, however unusual, might happen – a feeling of not being quite as firmly attached as usual to our surroundings. It was disorientating and exhilarating. At the same time we were walking through one of the most beautiful forested valleys in the Himalayas and breathing thin clear air, sweet with the sunny smell of pine resin.

Tapkhay was waiting for us outside a white-painted Sherpa house.

'They have very good apples here. Try one!' He pressed the apple he had been peeling into Julie's hand, and started working on a second.

'Lots of apple trees in this part of Solu.' He waved the apple and its trailing peel in the direction of the winter orchard behind the house, sheltered by the dark wall of the pine forest.

We sat munching apples for a while, and I tried to find words to describe to Julie the farms and villages snugged into clearings in the forest, the two- and three-storey houses, white-painted, with windows picked out in bright colours and the roofs grey-brown with pine shingles. Below us, in a field terraced into the hillside, a man pushed and guided his wooden plough through the dry winter earth, his hoarse shouts mingling with the sound of the bells around the necks of the two *zopkio** straining at the harness.

We crossed the river on an adequate but airy bridge of wire mesh, which Julie described as 'scary', and began the climb up the other side of the valley towards Thumbuk. Julie had been going well on the way down from Paphlu, but as soon as we started climbing she slowed right down and found she was getting short of breath every two or three minutes. As our rest stops became more and more frequent, I reminded myself that we were three thousand feet higher than Kathmandu now. There was no point in Julie becoming exhausted on the first day.

---

*zopkio (Sherpa): a cross between a yak and a cow, used both as a draft- and a pack-animal.

'Tapkhay, I don't think we're going to get to Thumbuk tonight.'

'No problem, no problem! This village up here is Salabesi, and you can stay at my uncle's house. Just keep going slowly, it's not very far.'

Julie had just announced that she couldn't walk another step when the house came into view around the corner. At this news she found an extra reserve of energy, and took the rest of the distance at a smartish trot. We ducked through the small but heavy wooden door.

'Hey, I think you should go first – it's pitch dark in here!'

'Who're you kidding? Use a torch or something.'

Tapkhay reappeared from an inner room with a flickering taper and guided us to seats by the open hearth. An old lady with white pigtails and striped apron brought a woollen rug to lay on the bench. We were in a large room with a plank floor and wooden benches around the wall. Behind the fire the wall was lined with shelves holding large copper cooking pots and brass bowls. The hearth itself was a raised square of clay in which three rocks were firmly placed supporting a bubbling pot of tea over a blazing twig fire.

The aged Sherpini handed us tea, then busied herself with the cooking pots. Lhakpa went out to the yard to erect the tents. Julie was almost asleep. Tapkhay chatted happily to anyone with enough energy to keep up. Huge piles of rice with spinach and potatoes were heaped onto our supper plates. Julie took to this better than she had to the salt tea, but was more interested in going to bed. I wondered if her tiredness was entirely to do with the altitude. She usually had much more energy than this.

Next morning Julie was more cheerful, but announced that she had a cold.

'Told you so. That's what comes of swanning around in your nothings in Kathmandu in winter.'

'No it isn't! I bet Kathmandu's *full* of germs.'

'Do you feel okay to go on today?'

'Oh yes; actually I don't feel as bad as I usually do with a cold. This must be a nice healthy place to get sick in.'

The way to Thumbuk was steep and the path little more than a line of footprints across a ploughed field. We were well off the main road for Sherpas, and certainly for trekkers. The Sherpas in these quiet villages live mainly by farming and herding – potatoes and barley, chickens and cattle . . . not much money, plenty of time.

Monks and villagers had carved great stones with prayers and mantras, and built them into 'mani' walls at intervals

along the trail. These marked good places for rest-stops, where Julie could get her fingers to work on the script. The most popular mantra, 'OM MANI PADME HUM', was that of Chenrezig, the Buddha of compassion.

In Tibetan script it would sometimes be repeated dozens of times on the same stone. I made Julie a cardboard cut-out of this back in England, so she was already familiar with the feel of the letters. Before long, her hands could decipher the mantra in all its different styles and sizes. I hoped she wouldn't wear her fingertips away on the rough granite in her enthusiasm for reading.

Thumbuk was little more than a small scattering of houses and farms; a watermill stood over a stream and the new gompa was perched above, on the hill.

'Come to my brother's house and have some tea.'

Tapkhay's brother was a carpenter. He had built a wooden extension to his house on the south side, with a glass window to let in the sun – a much warmer place to sit than within the thick stone walls of the house itself. Tapkhay himself is one of the best woodblock carvers in Nepal. A half-finished block was lying on the table by the window, and when I picked it up I was surprised at its weight. It was about eighteen inches square and an inch and a half thick, and was covered with elegant Tibetan script in black ink – in reverse, of course. Only the top half had been carved to bring the letters into relief. Julie ran her fingers over the carving and admired Tapkhay's skill and artistry. I remembered a story he once told me of a friend of his, a monk who lost his sight and learned to read the woodblocks like braille. To Julie this seemed very logical: use of her braille frame entailed writing a sentence in reverse, then flipping the card over to read the other side, forwards.

'It's taken me ten days so far, and it is only half finished. But I must finish it soon. It is for printing prayer flags. Then we'll have a big *puja** and put prayer flags all round the gompa!'

A jewelled horse was just emerging into relief in the centre of the text; the Sherpas call him *lung-ta,* the windhorse who carries on the wind the wisdom and blessings of the text to all the beings in the world.

'Come on, let me show you the gompa.'

**puja* (Nepali): ceremony involving meditation and recitation of prayers.

We followed a short, steep path up to the site of the new building. The Sherpinis had pitched the tents right outside the gompa on the crest of the ridge, by a tall prayer flag.

'You see, the block is printed over and over, the whole length of the flag,' explained Tapkhay.

We sat on the sunny ridge for a while, listening to the breeze rippling the white flag and the winter grass. Below us, in the valley, lay the village of Junbesi, and beyond, the white snow of Shorung Yu Lha, goddess of Solu. In spite of the half-finished building behind us, there was a sense of completeness and contentment about this place. It occurred to me that it would be nice to stop running up and down mountains for a while and to see if there was anything to be learned by standing still. Julie told me afterwards that she had a strong urge to return and spend more time here one day.

J ¶ There is an atmosphere of solitude and peace here. I can feel the space of the valley below us and see in my mind the villages, and the mountain above it all. I reached out to the slender tree-trunk supporting the prayer flag; it felt alive, vibrating with the wind. I like listening to Tapkhay's voice as he talks about his new gompa – so full of energy and enthusiasm, he easily inspires one with his vision of the place all finished and full of people. He speaks mostly in Nepali, with scattered bits of English surfacing from time to time. I wish I could understand Nepali instead of having to wait for it to be translated all the time. But such is the warmth of Tapkhay's personality he can establish a com-munication that is beyond words. This morning we gave him some money towards the building of his gompa. He couldn't have sounded more pleased if a king had just emptied out his treasury. ¶

We walked over to the new building, stepping over piles of rubble heaped outside, and the stacks of timber inside. Tapkhay's brother was working on the roof, fixing the last of the wooden shingles into place.

'When it's finished we'll paint it red on the outside, and all colours on the pillars and walls inside . . . pictures, like the ones in the gompa at Junbesi. And upstairs, a library.'

We scrambled up the rough wooden ladder to the bare planks of the second floor. Tapkhay's arm made an encompassing sweep of the stone-and-mortar walls and wooden floor as he described the finished building, the people who would come, and the scriptures he would teach.

'Do you have any good ideas for making it better? One friend suggested big windows so everyone can see the paintings and read the books easily – so you see, we're putting in big windows.'

I said, 'Why don't you have some cushions for the village people to sit on at puja time? In most gompas I've visited only the lamas have cushions, and the village people come along, make a few prostrations, then go home again. Maybe if they had something to sit on, they'd stay for the puja.'

Tapkhay roared with laughter. 'Good idea! Give them a comfortable seat and they'll stay . . . maybe we should give them sweets as well! Maybe sometimes trekkers will come as well? It would be nice to have some books in English as well as in Tibetan.'

A small boy scrambled up the ladder and handed Tapkhay a letter which had arrived at Junbesi post office the previous day. It was the letter I had written to him weeks before.

'Oh well, you got here anyway. Come and see the kitchen.'

The kitchen was no more than a makeshift wooden shelter on the hill behind the gompa. The carpenter was making the inevitable pot of tea. He passed the cups round, then sat back and lit up a cigarette. Tapkhay gave him a lecture on the evils of smoking. He looked thoughtfully at the cigarette in his hand.

'What to do? I didn't smoke until I worked with trekking groups, then the tourists gave me cigarettes. I'd like to stop now because it makes me cough, and my lama-brother says it is bad for my *Dharma** practice. But when I stop I feel really sick, so I start again.'

Dharma (Sanskrit): ethical precepts of Buddhism.

64

10 The bazar in Kathmandu.

11 Beginning the trek in Solu, with mountains of the Everest region in the distance.

12 Tapkhay's brother working on the roof of the new gompa in Thumbuk.

13 Tapkhay Lama and Julie in the makeshift kitchen of the gompa.

14 Julie reading the carved woodblock in Junbesi.

15 The village of Kunde.

16 Bridges without sides were
doubly difficult for Julie: the
sound of rushing water was
disorientating as she
negotiated the wobbly planks
underfoot.

17 Inside a Sherpa hotel.

Lhakpa quietly put out the cigarette he had been smoking and went outside to look for the Sherpinis.

That night Tapkhay slept in the gompa, and the next morning we were woken by the sound of chanting and bell-ringing as he made puja at dawn. At breakfast, he was looking pleased.

'First time I've slept in the gompa. It's nice to have the roof on. Last monsoon, I was up here on my own and the roof wasn't finished and the gompa started filling up with water. So there I was in the middle of the night, trying to bail it out by myself!'

Tapkhay wanted us to visit the monastery where he first studied, just outside Junbesi, so the Sherpinis were sent to meet Jangbu in the village itself, and to tell him we would be camping at the monastery instead of the village. The path down to the river was steep and muddy in places, and frequently Julie and I found ourselves slithering into each other, out of control. As we risked nothing worse than a mud-bath or a close encounter with a rhododendron bush, and the others felt free to enjoy the joke at our expense, it became a matter of personal pride to complete the descent in style. Even Tapkhay's nephew must have found it difficult with the heavy doko. By the time we were halfway down I noticed one of our tents strapped on top of Tapkhay's rucksack.

'Lhakpa, why aren't the Sherpinis carrying anything?'

'Oh, they'll carry after Junbesi.'

It did not seem proper to me that a respected lama should be carrying our junk. With the Sherpinis long gone, I offered to take it myself. Tapkhay refused, insisting we had enough problems of our own.

After we crossed the river to the sunny side of the valley, the path became drier and walking more straightforward. Above us the hillside, golden with dry grass, reared up to the bald rocks of the Lamijura Pass, over which we had skimmed in the tiny plane. Jangbu and his porters would be crossing the pass sometime today. We sat down to rest under a tall chir pine, the long needles scattered on the ground making a more comfortable seat than usual. I peeled apples while Julie examined a pine-cone. As soon as we had started going uphill she had begun to tire quickly again, and I wondered what she really thought about it all. Was she able to enjoy it in spite of her obvious exhaustion?

J ¶ It was so pleasant to sit back and soak in the sun. The breeze brought with it scents of dried grass and pine, and gentle hints of the herbs on the hillside, so much more pungent when crushed in my fingers. The pine-cones here are long and wide open, and are covered with sticky resin which I managed to get all over my hands and sweater. Resting times are when I can really appreciate my surroundings: going downhill, I have to concentrate on balance and placing my feet so they don't slip. It is obviously more tiring than if I could see where I was going, yet I don't seem to get unreasonably tired going down. But as soon as I start climbing, even though balancing is much easier, I feel as if I've been walking for a week without a rest! I suppose it's the effect of the altitude, which should wear off soon – and this wretched cold, which I hope will clear up soon as well.

Staying in Thumbuk was a wonderful experience – almost too much too soon. I found I could only just keep up with it all. I'm sure there are so many more exciting things waiting to happen further up the road; it would be awful to miss out on them because of a stupid cold. ¶

The last stretch up to the little white monastery was taken slowly, with Tapkhay walking a little ahead, giving encouragement, shaking his head and muttering '*Nyingje*' under his breath. This gentle Sherpa word means 'compassion' or 'sympathy'. He first used it to express his sympathy when Julie had tripped because of her blindness. Now it was simply because she was feeling exhausted.

The cluster of white-painted buildings sheltered in a grove of pine trees. As we approached I could see that our whole crew had met and arrived here. Baskets and boxes lay scattered around the entrance to the walled garden of the monastery. Suddenly voices were raised within, and the next minute

Jangbu and Dawa came scuttling through the gate clutching bits of camping equipment, with the Abbot in hot pursuit. Apparently they had started pitching tents on his front lawn without seeking permission. His Reverence had taken some exception to this, but once the offenders were safely out of the gardens, he beat a dignified retreat back to his house.

Tapkhay was apologetic. 'I'm sorry, I should have arrived here first and told him you were coming. Please have some tea in my house.'

The Sherpas slunk off to the village in search of a more acceptable campsite, while we drank tea in the little stone hut that had been Tapkhay's home during the years he had studied here. The room was barely twelve feet square, with whitewashed stone walls, two wooden benches and a small table. Woodblock prints of saints and deities were pasted around the walls, and a small altar stood in one corner. It was hard to imagine the kind of spartan existence people out here accept as part of life, while some will gladly undergo even harsher conditions in pursuit of spiritual attainments.

Tapkhay brought out another woodblock carved by a hermit who had lived in a cave in the mountains for many years. He had taught his skill to several devoted – and determined – students who had followed him up there. The block had been used to print large squares of cloth. Tapkhay gave Julie one of the cloth prints to keep. The wood was still inky enough to make her hands thoroughly black as she examined it, tracing her fingers around the delicately carved 'eight auspicious symbols'. For the first time she was able to 'read' for herself every detail of a picture she would never see.

We walked down to the village of Junbesi, and Tapkhay insisted on taking us on a tour of the village gompa. The temple itself stands within a courtyard surrounded by balconies, where the villagers gather to watch the temple dances every year. The carving on the pillars and doorways was the same as in the new gompa at Thumbuk, but here everything was painted in brilliant reds, blues and greens. Tapkhay was fiddling with the heavy iron lock, and with a bit of pushing the solid wooden door to the temple creaked open.

'Tell me what you can see,' whispered Julie.

'Nothing. It's very dark. I can see why Tapkhay wants big windows in his gompa.'

As my eyes adjusted to the gloom, the grandeur of the place came into focus around me. A huge seated Buddha statue some thirty feet high dominated the hall, flanked by statues of Chenrezig and Guru Rinpoche. On the altar before the statue stood heavy brass butter-lamps and a row of smaller water bowls. Tapkhay touched Julie's hand gently to the brimming bowls.

'At puja time we offer these. The Buddhas don't need what we offer them, they are beyond all that, but it is good for *our* minds if we do this practice.'

He led us to the seated figure of Guru Rinpoche, and with characteristic exuberance had us scrambling up on the seat by the wall. By reaching up as far as she could, Julie could just touch the petals of the lotus seat and a foot. She paused, her hands still on the cold painted surface of the statue.

'I've never seen anything as big as this. Suddenly I have to rearrange everything I've been seeing in my mind.'

The deep boom of a long Tibetan horn broke the silence; Tapkhay was demonstrating the sounds of the temple instruments. It takes years of practice to play the horns properly, but he encouraged us to try the heavy brass cymbals and the huge leather drum hanging from a beam. The sides of the drum were carved and painted like the pillars and the shelves containing the volumes of Buddhist scriptures. Each volume comprised long narrow sheaves of parchment printed from woodblocks, smaller versions of those we had already seen. Each parchment volume was wrapped in a piece of silk, then bound between two blocks of wood to keep it flat. Two hundred volumes lined the walls; Tapkhay said they came from Tibet.

Our footsteps echoed on the bare boards of the hall, cold and quiet like an empty stage. At puja time it would be so different, lit by the glow of hundreds of butter-lamps and filled with the sound of chanting and instruments, while the little novice monks scuttled around with the big sooty kettles keeping everyone supplied with tea. This vision made the present silence more intense by comparison, yet there was a powerful presence that went beyond the echoes and the smell of incense and butter.

Outside in the sun, the prayer flag fluttered in the centre of the paved courtyard, and beyond, in the village, children were playing. Our tents looked bright and incongruous in the corner of a fallow potato field. Smoke was rising from a wooden shelter nearby.

Tapkhay walked with us to the centre of the village.

'I must go home now. I still have a lot of work to do. But I have to go to Kathmandu in a few weeks, so I will see you there.' He draped kataks around our necks. 'I am so happy you came to visit me – you know, you are the first tourist-people to see my new gompa!'

He strode away up the hill, turning to wave once before disappearing round a shoulder of the hillside. The sun set behind the ridge of the Lamijura, engulfing the village in chill evening shadow and hurrying our steps towards the camp. Time spent in Tapkhay's company always goes too quickly for me; he sweeps you up in his enthusiasm and your ideas are hard put to keep up with him. He has a cheerful disregard for any ostentatious piety, yet conversations with him are always thought-provoking, pieces surfacing like little bubbles in the memory for days afterwards.

Jangbu had cooked an enormous supper, a gastronomic feast in contrast to the simple fare we had been eating in the villages. Julie gave up less than halfway through.

'I'm sorry, Jangbu. It's delicious, but I'm really not used to eating so much.'

'Why sorry? No problem!' He cleared away the plates and rejoined the rest of the crew in the smoky cookhut.

It was too cold and dark to do much but retreat to the tents. I lay for a long time without sleeping. Although she was playing it down, I knew Julie's cold was getting worse, and was probably the reason for her eating less than usual. Perhaps this was also why she seemed to be acclimatising so slowly. We were no higher than nine thousand feet and she was tiring as quickly as she had on the first day. If she really was so badly affected at this altitude, there seemed little chance she would be able to cope with the additional eight thousand feet we needed to gain in order to reach Base Camp. On the other hand, to put it down to the cold was no more encouraging: I knew how bad Julie's coughs and colds could become – and how long they could last. She was well into her bottle of cough medicine already, and was still getting worse. Most people find it more difficult to recover from an illness at high altitude, and I was concerned that she should overcome the worst of it while we were still relatively low. I had to admit that I was more apprehensive about Julie's health on this trip than I was about her blindness. I caught myself feeling disappointed that she might not be able to enjoy the journey as much as I had imagined she would, and wondered if I, too, had preconceived ideas of how everything should be.

So often people asked me, 'Don't you feel it's a terrible responsibility taking a blind person on a trip like this?' Taking a relatively inexperienced person into the mountains is always a responsibility, but no one comments on that under normal circumstances. Julie and I saw things a little differently: our partnership had bridged the gap between 'the helpless handicapped' and what is supposedly 'normal'. Yet there was no denying that doubts expressed by such people as our recalcitrant insurance company had had the effect of nibbling away at our self-confidence. Was this journey foolhardy? If we had to beat an untimely retreat back to England, there would be plenty of people ready to say 'We told you so.'

5

The Witches

The morning sun comes late to Junbesi, nestled in its deep wooded valley, and everyone was slow to get packed and organised.

'Lhakpa, how many porters do we have now? There seem to be an awful lot of people hanging about.'

'Ah, two Rai people and two Sherpinis.'

I watched for a while as the loads were hefted onto the backs of the four Rais who had arrived with Jangbu from Jiri.

'So *how* many porters do we have?'

'Ah. Four Rais, and two Sherpinis.'

'But the Sherpinis aren't carrying anything.'

'Yes. Well. They will carry after Kharikhola.'

'You said that about Junbesi.'

Lhakpa shuffled his feet, then looked up and smiled disarmingly.

'Don't worry, I'll tell them tonight.'

I wondered how long he was going to string this out. The Sherpinis were probably relatives of his enjoying some fringe benefits of having a Sirdar in the family. I was beginning to perceive Lhakpa's Western manners and clothes as indicative of opportunist motives. He was probably hoping he could charm his way out of trouble if I became too suspicious. This situation was all too similar to the one I had encountered during the last season's guiding, and I was in no mood for a repeat performance. This would never have happened with Ang Dorjee . . . I paused. I had carefully put all thoughts of Ang Dorjee away in a quiet corner of my mind, until time would make them less painful. It was still too soon, I decided, and pushed them back into the shadows again. I would have to deal with his replacement as best I could and try not to make comparisons.

The trail wound up the little ridge to the east of Junbesi, crossing several small streams by means of stepping-stones through the resulting bog. Frost still lay on the ground, so it seemed a good idea to keep one's feet dry rather than wallow through the mud. It was a severe test of verbal directions, with Julie teetering on a slippery rock while I tried to give her accurate co-ordinates for the next perch. To give them their due, the Sherpinis were most concerned for Julie's well-being and did their utmost to help her across these awkward stretches. Even so, they seemed unable to 'tune in' to what Julie was trying to do. They would both grab her spare hand (the one that was not holding mine) and then try to lift her by the arm, which had the effect of pulling her over. Julie felt constrained by politeness to offer no more comment than 'thank you', while I silently determined that these young ladies, sweet as they might be, were an expensive luxury without which we were soon going to be having a much easier time. During this erratic progress it became clear that, contrary to what we had planned, there would be no time when Julie could take a turn at walking with one of the staff. Neither of us felt confident to try the experiment in these conditions, where there was often a drop of ten feet or more below the path. It made us realise how much we relied on an intuitive communication between us, and that this gained strength from what we had already experienced together. Julie tried to put it into words for her tape-recorder.

J ¶ The most difficult thing is just to keep one's balance. Often rocky steps are formed by boulders piled higgledy-piggledy on top of one another, and it is all too easy to step on a 'wobbler' the wrong way and twist an ankle, especially when going downhill. But Elaine is a very good and patient guide, and I feel safe with her, even in the most tricky situations. What amazes me is that she manages to stay even-tempered at times when I must be very trying. I asked her about it the other day, and she admitted that once or twice she had felt a bit cross after seeing me making the same mistake again and again, but she had caught herself feeling negative and realised that I wasn't doing it on purpose. I've noticed how our reactions depend on our moods. When everything is going well and we are in good spirits, mishaps and discomforts are passed off almost unnoticed. If your blood sugar is low, even the smallest irritation assumes ridiculous proportions. I certainly wouldn't trust myself with anyone else, so it looks as if we're stuck with each other whether we like it or not!

We are settling into a routine now: Dawa brings hot water for washing in the mornings – oh, what luxury, except that the air is so cold you don't want to put your nose outside the sleeping-bag.

This morning we were discussing the way ahead, how fast we have been travelling, and likely camping places. I knew at once there was something Elaine avoided. Bit by bit, it came out that she was trying to work it so that we didn't end up camping in a village called Manidingma, where some friends of hers had once been given poisoned food. It seems there are witches in the village who try to poison you so that your ghost becomes their slave. I don't think I want to camp there either!

Days on the road are long, but there are plenty of tea-shops at which to stop. The tea-shops would be mistaken for sheds in England, often no more than one-room plank affairs, with a Sherpini brewing tea in a sooty pot over an open fire. I can't say I've developed a taste for the Tibetan salt tea which is usually served, and I've always disliked sweetened tea. I am pampered in camp with black

73

tea without sugar, but Elaine assures me that as we gain altitude I shall start to crave more sugar.

The 'hotels' are a little grander, usually a private house whose owner has taken the notion to feed passing porters and trekkers with tea, rice and vegetables, or boiled potatoes. There isn't much else to eat. Travellers can sleep the night on the wooden benches on which they have sat to eat, and this comes free with the meal. I'm glad we are camping because it would be very difficult for me to find my way around a strange place each night. In my own tent, I know where all my things are located, and I can be almost independent. The blue nylon string from Kathmandu is an essential item of equipment. In the evening, Elaine fixes a guideline from my tent pole to the loo tent. Then I try out the route with her before going solo.

It worried me at first to think that everyone was going slowly to suit my pace. Elaine just laughed and said, 'Why? I'd be going just as slowly to take photographs, and if it wasn't for us the Sherpas wouldn't be doing this at all. *They're* not trying to get to anywhere.' Now I'm getting used to the idea that the pace here is not that of London.

We walk until we arrive at camp shortly before sunset at about six o'clock. Woe betide the extremities of anyone caught outside a sleeping-bag after the sun has gone. I don't like getting my fingers cold and numb, because I can't 'see' anything until they thaw out again. Last night I spent the time alternately dozing and enjoying the night sounds and the river rushing down the valley. It is all so different from my usual environment in London that being wakeful doesn't bother me. I very much enjoy the quietness. ¶

Out of the valley, the sun warmed the dry grass and the path became easier. We could look down on the changing colours of the forest, while high on the opposite hill the stone walls of Tapkhay's new gompa caught the sunlight. Walking was pleasant in the sun and breeze, the pace was moderate, and rest-stops plentiful. Conversations at rest-stops ranged from the profound to the inane.

'Elaine, have you got the shampoo with you? I want to wash my hair at lunchtime.'

'Not till your cold's better. It's still freezing cold out of the sun.'

'Pooh, you're horrid! I shall feel awful till I've washed it.'

'Get better quick then.'

Pause.

'What are you laughing about?'

'Oh, I don't know really. It's just nice to sit in the sun, listening to the river . . . the trees are turning yellow . . . '

'My face is turning red . . . '

'Oh no! It had better not be, you'll upset all my photographs! Put some suncream on.'

'Mm, now where did I put it . . . maybe I'll go black just to annoy you – black as the witch of Manidingma's hat.'

'I'm not sure they have hats like that out here . . . maybe it's just hearsay anyway . . . Lhakpa, have you ever stayed in Manidingma?'

'No, we don't stay there. Sometimes we camp there with a trekking group, but we don't buy food in the village.'

'Why not?'

'Because you die. No-good people there.'

'Maybe that's just more hearsay.'

'Don't think I feel like camping there anyway,' said Julie.

That evening Lhakpa went to have his talk with the Sherpinis. He returned with the news that they had decided to visit Kathmandu instead, as they had never been there. I was relieved; they were going on a spree, so I could feel less mean about my efforts to save our budget. Lhakpa seemed happy with the solution, although it was difficult to tell what he was thinking. He was careful to maintain an unruffled attitude to everything, always ready with a smile and a joke. He gave the impression of speaking perfect English, but I was beginning to notice he would lapse into Nepali if he thought he might make mistakes in the English. I was becoming concerned that we were so often at cross purposes. Our success and safety depended a great deal on Lhakpa's constructive help and co-operation.

Next morning breakfast was late. By the time I reached the cookhut the porters were already on the road, except one who had been kept behind to wait for the tents. Suspicious, I went to look up the road, in time to see the two Sherpinis disappearing – away from Kathmandu – with dokos on their backs.

'I thought you said they were going to Kathmandu?'

'Well, they were . . . then they realised they didn't have enough money, so . . . '

'How many porters do we have today?'

'Ah. Four Rais and two Sherpinis.'

'So today six people are carrying what four people carried yesterday!'

'Well, it's only to Lukla. Then we can get zopkios.'

'But we are travelling very slowly. It will be five or six days to Lukla. We can't afford to pay and feed two extra people we don't need. Brian said they would get their own food like the other porters, but every time I go in the kitchen, I find them eating our food.'

With a great show of perplexity, Lhakpa took the staff and equipment list from Jangbu, and studied it carefully. I assured him that Brian had insisted we needed only three staff, not five. Poor Lhakpa. He'd probably promised them a nice holiday around the villages.

'I'll tell them tonight.'

I felt like an executioner. I did not want to spoil their fun, but at the same time I was determined to ensure they did not take advantage. My thoughts panned briefly to the incorruptible Ang Dorjee, then flitted away again.

The morning was crisp and clear and beautiful, too beautiful to be spoiled by worries and arguments. I realised that I resented the intrusion of the hassle into my peaceful morning more than the cause of the hassle itself. What an exemplary exercise in futility!

We passed the Taksindo cheese factory just below the top of the pass. Lhakpa said there was a wide cobbled trail straight down the valley from here to Paphlu; porters would carry the cheese to the airstrip, whence it would be flown in the tiny Pilatus to Kathmandu with its tourist delicatessens.

'Always hard to get seat from Paphlu to Kathmandu because planes are full of cheese.'

Most of the local farmers must be selling their milk here for cash; the only milk you see in Solu these days is dried milk powder from India.

From the top of the pass the great valley of the Dudh Kosi river spread out below our feet. Beyond were the mountains of Khumbu, white and beautiful, but still tantalisingly distant. A chill wind was blowing from the snow mountains, nipping through our clothes and stirring the prayer flags and kataks on the cairn at the crest of the pass. A few yards away, on a small area of flat ground, a great stone chörten stood silhouetted against the bright snow of Shorung Yu Lha. Julie and I walked around the square base of it, about fifteen feet on each side. Somehow it did not seem quite respectful to go scrambling up it for a feel around, so we sat at the bottom while I described the stone sphere above the square, and the long slender spire supporting a sun and moon, glinting gold in the sunlight. Each section of the chörten represents one of the five elements: earth, water, air, fire and space, but the symbolism goes deeper, and invites years of study to be fully understood.

Once over the pass, the trail descended in broad zigzags stepped with earth packed behind horizontal pine logs. Wild giant rhododendrons reared forty and fifty feet into the air on each side of us. Three martens were playing and feeding in a tree above, slinky and graceful, seemingly unconcerned by their audience. Taksindo gompa basked quietly in the thin sunshine; the lama had gone away for the Mani Rimdu festival at Chiwong.

We could feel the air gradually becoming warmer as we descended, and far below us the distant roar of the Dudh Kosi became audible.

Suddenly Julie said, 'Lhakpa told me it would be another hour to Manidingma, but we're there already!'

'How did you know? I didn't tell you. I'd decided not to.'

'There's no need! I don't like at all the way it feels here; it's heavy and oppressive, as if there's going to be a storm . . . as though there are eyes everywhere, watching you.'

It was the only village we had visited where the children laughed and pointed rudely at Julie as we passed. A fat woman drying corn on a bamboo mat stared unsmilingly, and an old man gathering cow fodder squinted at us through half-closed eyes.

We caught up with Jangbu and the porters taking a rest at the far end of the village.

'You going to i-stop for some tea?' asked Jangbu mischievously.

'Not if I was dying of thirst!' said Julie, with feeling.

Even Lhakpa's laugh had a brittle edge to it as we turned and followed the road out of the village.

It was a long descent to the river and Julie seemed to be in good spirits. Whether it was the dramatic loss of altitude or the antibiotics she had started taking yesterday, neither of us could tell, but she kept getting ahead of me as we walked, and I would sometimes find myself running to keep up.

'Hey! Where do you think you're going?'

'Well, it's like this, you see. I'm in a hurry to get to Everest and was getting bored walking slowly with you.'

'I'm sure Bruno doesn't have this problem – or do you go running on ahead of him too?'

'Oh, all right, I'll behave. Poor Bruno wouldn't be much help out here, I'm afraid. Apart from not being trained to guide out in the country, he really is quite the old gentleman with rheumaticky legs. He'd be puffing and flaking out on the uphills more than me. It's very . . . oops!'

'Oh no, not again. Slow *down*!'

'No damage done. I just seem to have very slack tendons in my ankles and they turn easily. I used to have terrible problems with my ankles, always spraining them. Perhaps that's why they're so weak.'

'How come you didn't tell me any of this before we got out here?'

'Thought it might put you off.'

'Dead right. Hey, d'you mind me mentioning that you're suffering from brake failure again?'

In the end Julie did twist her ankle, but after a few minutes of hobbling she decided it was not serious and resumed walking. The long day was taking its toll, rests grew more frequent, and before long she was declaring she could go no further. The edge in her voice told me she meant it. These announcements of imminent collapse had been christened 'fifty-yard squeaks' for they came every time with uncanny accuracy only fifty yards from the camp. Julie said that if she could see how far we had to go it wouldn't happen, but even though I could see, and had been this way before, I had only an approximate idea of how far we still had to go each day. I could not remember every twist and turn of the trail through the forest. In any case, I could not know just where the Sherpas up ahead would choose to make camp.

We dropped down steeply towards the river below a gravel cliff. The distant grumbling of the water had become a powerful roar, which became almost deafening as we edged round the cliff face on a narrow parapet to reach the bridge. The bright turquoise water foamed as it rushed below the wire mesh of the bridge; to watch it too long was to lose your balance and grab at the sides. The wire was strung with prayer flags, kataks, and marigolds – offerings from both Buddhists and Hindus for a safe crossing of that terrible water.

From a flat area between great boulders on the river bank, smoke was drifting up between the leaves of the forest. The air was warm and humid at this, the lowest point of the whole trek. Jangbu was waiting for us in characteristic pose, head on one side, looking at us quizzically, kettle in one hand.

'Okay? Tea?'

Julie sat down and leaned against a boulder, thankful to have arrived. 'Oh Jangbu, you are a little wonder! I'm going to smuggle you home in my rucksack. Do you think you'll fit?'

Jangbu was not so sure, but he just grinned and shrugged and went back to his cooking pots.

There was a shout from the trail above our camp site; the Sherpinis were leaving.

79

'Going home,' said Lhakpa solemnly.

I felt relief tinged with disappointment. The Sherpinis had been fun with their constant silly giggles, but they had not been able to help Julie much and they were expensive . . . At least there would be no cause now for daily disputes with our Sirdar. The Sherpinis had done quite well out of us. I hoped Lhakpa would not feel resentful that they had to leave before Lukla.

I went over to the cook-fire for some more tea. Jangbu was watching the retreating Sherpinis.

'What to do? They just weren't strong, and couldn't carry.' Jangbu seemed much older when he was speaking fluent Nepali instead of broken English. Even his sixteen-year-old looks seemed to change subtly as I watched him evaluating the situation. He continued, 'I think there was a mix-up with the message that was sent to Lhakpa in Lukla. *I* know that Brian said they should be porters, but Lhakpa was under the impression he had to bring two nice Sherpinis to help with Julie.'

Poor Lhakpa. Having just arrived with two nice Sherpinis for escort, he is told insistently that they must carry thirty-kilo loads. Rather than admit a mistake, he tries to solve the problem with his own brand of clumsy diplomacy – which I then interpret as devious trickery. I realised I had been allow-ing the misdoings of my previous Sirdar to affect my judge-ment. Perhaps I had been prejudiced against Lhakpa simply because he was not Ang Dorjee.

Lhakpa came into the 'kitchen' looking for his cigarettes.

'Oh, Lhakpa, I'm sorry about the Sherpinis.'

'Why sorry?' He grinned cheerfully. 'You know, I think my cigarettes must have dropped out of my pocket up the road.'

Evidently not a man to harbour a grudge.

That night I could hear Julie coughing, even above the roar of the river.

I awoke with clinging memories of strange dreams of islands in a swirling mass of water and great crocodiles heaving themselves out of the mud to lie in wait for the unwary.

Above the camp, a line of porters trudged past in the dawn mist carrying bundles of hides to trade in the weekly market at Namche Bazar. Behind them, the jungle reared up against the dawn, damp and green and alive with things that chirp and croak. It is Nepal's lifeblood, an animal growing from the hillside; you can feel its rhythm and power beside the growl of the river.

Julie was moody and sluggish. The heavy air affected her and she hated the constant noise of the river. Soon we were climbing steeply out of the gorge to the easier slopes above, where the jungle had been almost completely cleared for firewood, for building, for farmland. It is not that Nepalis fail to understand that in destroying the forest they are destroying the future fertility of their land – they understand it all too well – but what to do? There are many mouths to feed, meals to cook . . . and so the nibbling at the edges of the forest continues year by year. Great swathes of the hillside were covered by neat terraces separated by patches of low scrub.

The village of Jubing is inhabited mainly by Rais; their white-painted thatched cottages are interspersed with just a few red-ochred houses of the Chettri-Bahuns, the high-caste Hindus. Julie noticed immediately how different this village felt to the Sherpa villages of Solu – the warm, damp air and the smell of lush green plants everywhere. Tall stands of bamboo shaded the houses, some covered with creeping yscous vines which had escaped from a nearby rooftop.

Jangbu and Dawa were bargaining for yscous with a skinny Rai villager who was already perched on his roof, curved sickle at the ready. The bargain struck, the spiky green pear-shaped vegetables were tossed down and Dawa gathered them gingerly up to stash them in his doko among the cooking pots and tea-kettles. I wondered if the villagers shinned up the bamboos in pursuit of the runaway vines.

The gentle village sounds drifted over to us as we walked through: the chatter of neighbours from one terrace to another, the steady *thud, thud* of a hand-thresher from inside a cottage, a clutch of tiny chicks cheeping and pecking beneath an upturned doko, and the constant assertive call of the village roosters. Had I noticed such detail of sound before I knew Julie? It was hard to dissociate myself from the present and remember past perceptions.

Bright orange marigolds were growing everywhere in the village. Julie was delighted, her fingers tracing the delicate double petals while her mind created great swathes of them around her. There was more to explore: the golden clusters of drying corn cobs stacked outside the houses, the crimson spikes of amaranthus in the fields, and the innocent-looking little white flowers with their devilish hooked seed-pods that get inextricably tangled up in your socks. We scrambled up to a field of ripening millet. Julie said the curly heads of grain were like hands, and for the first time I saw a field full of little brown hands, their curly fingers reaching for the sun.

Lhakpa was waiting to urge us to stop for tea at the village post office and tea-shop. We needed no persuasion. He was talking with three young monks who were returning to their monastery at Pang Kwam Ma, Lhakpa's home village, high on the ridge above our route. The conversation revolved round Lhakpa's questions about what was happening in the village, and I wondered how long it was since he had been home.

Some porters were cooking up their morning meal on the road beside the tea-shop, and the smoke from the twig fires drifted over. I could tell they were making diro because of the heavy mixing with a wooden spatula. Diro is usually made from ground and toasted millet grain, and when boiled thickens to a kind of mud. In my experience, it also tastes and digests like mud, and is the only Nepalese food I really cannot eat, but it is, I am told, very nutritious and can be cooked in a few minutes over a tiny twig fire. Two men were trying to navigate a large grey bisi (water buffalo) between the cook-pots and fires, causing chaos as it tried to poke its snout into the pots as it passed. One of the porters fetched it a resounding swat on the rump with a large twig, and it took off up the road with the two men at pains to keep up. We followed, but at a more leisurely pace – at least until Julie discovered she was feeling better today and refused to rest until we were both gasping for breath.

'We're right above the Dudh Kosi gorge now . . . phew! I don't know why I'm trying to talk to you while I'm still gasping. Whose idea was it to run?'

'Whose idea was it to come here in the first place?'

'I'm not sure . . . but when you find out, let me know and I'll shoot whoever it was . . . Watch out, trough ahead.'

A 'trough' was a water run-off ditch broadside across the path, usually no more than a foot wide but easy for Julie to trip over if she had no warning. Our hand communications had become more refined: a complex series of twitches and squeezes which complemented an almost instinctive sensitivity to each other's body movements. It had become a nuisance having to take my pack off at every single-file section, and Lhakpa suggested it would be easier for him to carry it all the time. The three of us cut down our daytime needs to little more than a jacket and cameras, stuffed into my pack which Lhakpa carried. Even so, it was heavier than the load Sirdars are usually expected to carry, and I thought it was very public-spirited of him to volunteer. It was hard at first for me to get used to not having the cameras with me every time I wanted them, and there were occasionally other inconveniences.

'I wonder where Lhakpa is with the chocolate?'

'You little oink! You've only just had breakfast. Grunt of the Day award for you.'

'Look who's talking! Who confessed only this morning to waking up in the night and scoffing a whole bar single-handed? You're heading straight for the Golden Trough of the Year!'

We both knew the haranguing was just an expression of relief that Julie was at last getting her appetite back.

We passed the two men and their misbehaving bisi having breakfast by the side of the road, the men eating diro with their fingers and the bisi munching into a switch of leafy sal twigs. The Dudh Kosi gorge was well below us now, Taksindo perched on its ridge far behind us, and the snow mountains no more than little white snouts disappearing behind the shoulder of the hill ahead. The world changes shape as you move; sometimes the horizontal perspective is lost, sometimes the vertical. It depends on where you are looking from, whether your eyes are deceived by the light or the mist, or, perhaps, what you are looking for in the first place. Who can say if one reality is more valid than another? Was mine any more valid than the one Julie was creating in her mind from my clumsy descriptions? Would I ever learn to be aware of the subtleties of sound and smell that her finely-tuned senses perceived?

We came to another wire suspension bridge over a large tributary. It had stout sides, and Julie wanted to try it alone. I was tempted; it would make some good pictures. She set off, gripping the sides and edging forward carefully on the swaying bridge. Before she was halfway across, a group of ragged children playing on the far side spied her uncertain step and ran shrieking onto the bridge, shaking and swinging it to try to unbalance her. I ran forward to steady her, and shouted angrily at the children to get out of her way. They just stood and stared at us, grubby faces open-mouthed, and I continued to berate them until they scuttled off back to their mothers working in the terraced fields. I felt really shaken, and also guilty for letting Julie try it alone. Such mindless and spiteful behaviour is unusual in the children up here, where they grow up as part of a close community and their sense of responsibility towards others is usually very mature. But then, every community has its reprobates; it's just unfortunate if you come across them halfway across a wobbly bridge.

The episode was a sharp reminder of the tight margin between success and disaster. At any minute a pleasant walk in the sun could become an emergency involving a sprained ankle, illness, a fall from a bridge or cliff. The more serious possibilities were uncomfortable even to think about. Apart from the distances to be covered each day, and the altitude, there was nothing exceptionally rugged about this first part of the trek – for those with sight. Julie not only had to adjust her body to the continuous walking and the rarefied air; she had the added exertion of keeping her balance on the rock-strewn trail. It must surely also have been mentally tiring to know there was always potentially a cliff or drop somewhere near at hand. One thing I found impressive was that, as well as dealing with all this, she still managed to remain far tidier than I did, with a spotless white jumper, and her hair always in place.

It was a long climb from the bridge in the hot sun, dusty and dry, and Lhakpa was still out of sight with the snacks and water. Below us, a curved terrace of winter wheat glowed brilliant green in the afternoon sun, while a rooster perched on a wooden shed shone red and gold. A wrinkled Sherpini with gold earrings and a missing tooth sat outside her house weaving a doko from green bamboo strips.

'Come on. She says you can come and look. Don't get poked by the ends sticking out.'

The woman held out the half-woven basket for Julie to feel. It was light enough to hold on one finger, yet so intricately woven it would carry thirty kilos.

'Can't her eyes see at all? Can her ears hear?'

I translated for Julie, who assured the woman in English that she could hear very well, and liked talking to people. This needed no return translation, and we all laughed.

'How does she go along the road?'

'We go together.'

'How far are you going? Up to the snow?'

'Yes, to the snow. To Pheriche and Lobuche. Have you been there?'

'No, not me, I've never been right up there.'

'Come with us.'

'Aah, too far for me!'

A little further up, strips of green bamboo were soaking in a stream to make them pliable enough to weave.

The chörten on the ridge marked the end of the day's walking, but none of the crew had yet arrived. Not that it mattered much, as we sat outside the little teashop, swinging our feet over the edge of the terrace, trying to drink too-hot tea, and watching the afternoon fade on the river far below. There were straw mats spread around the chörten with heads of millet drying, and a woman on guard with an armoury of little pebbles to defend her harvest from a farrow of marauding piglets.

6

Chang

'My goodness, you were slow!' said Julie with exaggerated scorn as the crew arrived.

Jangbu and Dawa grinned, unabashed, and began setting up their kitchen in the back of the tea-shop. It was clear they had worked in plenty of camp kitchens before. No time or energy was wasted as they set out the bags and packets of dried food on sheets of plastic, stoked up the fire, and put a sooty dixie of water on to boil for tea. In spite of the confined space, there was no jostling or confusion as they moved about. Jangbu, small and nimble, seemed able to flit between Dawa's heavy, lumbering movements, while issuing cryptic instructions on today's menu at the same time. Dawa said little, usually answering with his now familiar lop-sided grin.

Lhakpa sauntered over, looking pleased with himself.

'Two new porters. Sherpa porters, with good clothes. They can go up where it's cold and no problems. This is my brother Kaji. He's brought a tape of Sherpa songs. I thought you'd like to hear it.'

Lhakpa is one of those people with the knack of getting you mad and then defusing you before you have a chance to say anything. Two of the Rai porters were being paid off and would go back in the morning. Kaji was only seventeen, but solidly built, like a yak.

'He's carried thirty kilos to the top of Mera Peak,' boasted Lhakpa on his brother's behalf. The other boy, Mingmar, was more slightly built, and quieter, rather in Kaji's shadow.

I looked across at Pang Kwam Ma as it caught the sun's rays on the ridge high above us.

'You didn't go all the way up there did you?'

Lhakpa shook his head. 'No. My family have another house, a smaller one, down in Kharikhola. Kaji was there.'

Julie was rummaging through her luggage and pulled out the two books on guide dogs she had been given by the Guide Dogs for the Blind Association.

'You said you were telling them about "dog-school" last night and they still think it's a joke? We should show them these, then they'll have to believe it!'

So we went through the books carefully, page by page; I gave a commentary to the photographs while Julie added anecdotes of her own. Lhakpa translated into Sherpa for the villagers who were gathering, some of whom spoke little Nepali. The whistles and mutterings of amazement brought Jangbu and Dawa out of their kitchen, and we had to start the story over again.

'Blind people can go to work. Some of them have good jobs in schools and offices; they go to work with their dogs.'

'Getting off the train, the dog looks to see if the way is clear before it walks.'

'At the road, if a car is coming, it sits and waits until it's clear, then it crosses.'

'The puppies come to the school to be trained – you thought I was joking didn't you?' (Much laughter.)

'They have to learn not to jump over things because a person might not be able to follow them.'

Julie said, 'Bruno still jumps puddles and makes me walk through them.'

'And they have to learn only to eat when they're told, and not to get angry if food is taken away.'

This was the picture that caused the most surprise – four

dogs with their food bowls in front of them, waiting to be told to eat – so different to the scavenging, desperate dogs in Nepal.

'How about this one for dog-school?' The tea-shop lady brought out a tiny black puppy and handed it to Julie, who spent the next half-hour cooing with delight over the wriggling bail of fluff.

'Aren't you lovely . . . ooh, sweetie-pie, you're so little . . . '

It would be useless to warn her about fleas and dermatitis; Bruno was thousands of miles away, in another life.

Next day, we dug out the rope. Lhakpa said the bad stretch of the trail had recently been repaired after two Rai porters fell to their deaths. Still, I was taking no chances. What might be a major highway for the nimble Lhakpa might be a major disaster for Julie and me.

The first warning of the difficulties ahead came with the cliffs of banded white and gold rock into which the trail had been cut. As we climbed higher, the ground dropped away below us so steeply that the distant river became audible again. The road itself had been shored up with great walls of intricate stonework which held it suspended, as it were, against the cliff face. The sun still warmed the rocks here, and Julie and I amused ourselves examining the crumbly stone glinting with fools' gold, while I silently tried to banish misgivings about the frost and ice ahead.

Ahead of us, the road twisted up round the shoulder of a ridge so steeply that it appeared to rise above the summits of the distant mountains. There was only blue sky beyond the corner where it turned, as if we would be walking off the edge of the world. We rounded the shoulder to the north side, into a winter place of shadow and hoar-frost, breath smoking in the sharp air. Everything now changed: we walked carefully, shoes crunching in the thick frost, slipping unexpectedly on treacherous patches of ice hidden beneath leaves or dirt. The cliff below the path fell away to the river and I kept as far from that side as possible on the narrow trail. Above us, a wall of rock and earth rose up, blocking out the sun. A few gnarled trees clung to crevices in the cliff, while below us there were clumps of small bamboos and grass interspersed with the grey, steep rock. There was not enough vegetation to muffle the ominous rumble of the river far below, and the sound was a constant reminder of our airy position.

'I hope you don't mind me telling you about the drop. At least you know you can relax at other times.'

'I can tell anyway because of the way the sounds resonate. But it's good to be reminded to concentrate more in places where it matters.'

Lhakpa watched carefully, going in front on icy stretches to brace himself and support us as we came down. Ahead, the path was cut by the rocky gash of a monsoon-time torrent, which had swept earth, plants and the road into the river below. Now, in winter, all water was frozen on the mountain high above. Only the rocky chasm remained. Lhakpa stood at the edge, feet firmly planted, ready to grab us if we slipped.

'Two Rai people died down there.'

I looked down the yawning hole of ice and rock, and shivered. Last time I had crossed, it had been by means of meagre hand- and foot-holds on a rockface glazed with ice. It seemed a pity that two people had had to fall to their doom before anyone got around to fixing it. Now, a kind of tunnel had been hollowed out of the cliff, and slabs and splinters of rock had been roughly levelled underfoot. The chipped-out roof curved over just above our heads, and the third side of the 'tunnel' opened out into space. Lhakpa was whistling a tuneless dirge which echoed eerily from the frosty rocks. It was true, we would not need the rope if we were careful. But once across, the path was exposed on the edge of nothing, with no respite from the frost and ice. It was frustrating to have to move so slowly and carefully when the cold made you want to run to keep warm.

I lost track of time in an endless succession of crunching, slithering footsteps, until we reached the avalanche. A vast lump of the cliff had fallen away, leaving a great amphitheatre of tumbled rocks and boulders, unstable and poised for a further slip. The road here was little more than a temporary rearrangement of what had already come down, weaving between blocks the size of a truck. It was hard for Julie, as she found heavy boulders suddenly rocking under her feet. Cracks opened up in front of us and our feet dislodged rocks which tumbled into the chute below with a cold, echoing rattle. I shall never forget the sound of those rocks: hollow, unearthly, as if we were trespassing on a piece of the underworld accidentally exposed to the surface.

A stray shaft of sunlight caught a patch of mossy rocks on the far side, and we edged into the warmth for a rest. It was not so much our limbs that had become fatigued as our concentration. Then we plunged back again into the cold shadows.

'When we've crossed this tributary we'll be back in the sun. Now you've got a choice: there's a real bridge, made of wood, with real sides, or there's the "pretend bridge" at the side of it made of two rotten logs.'

'I'll take the real one with sides, thank you – but don't let me spoil your fun. You can go and play on the rotten logs if you want to . . . '

The wooden planks and handrails were barely clear of the splashes from the roaring waterfall that plunged into a cauldron of shiny rocks below the bridge. In spite of the cold, Julie hovered there for a while, enjoying the powerful noise of the water.

'So long as it's only for a few minutes.'

A crowd of porters had stopped for a snack in the first patch of sunshine on the opposite bank, perched on warm rocks like a great flock of birds come home to roost. We passed to the sound of multiple crunching and the aroma of toasted corn.

'What's up with these memsahibs?'

'*Raksi lagyo*,' teased Lhakpa. 'They're drunk – ten bottles!'

I could see some of them still looking puzzled. We might be holding on to each other, but surely we didn't have quite the rolling stagger of inebriates.

There was a stone hut higher on the sunny side of the hill.

The proprietress, an ancient Sherpini with a stoop and hands blackened and calloused from the potato fields, made 'ready-mix' tea that came straight from the kettle, with the milk and sugar already in. Even Julie was quite content to drink it. We sat for a long time watching a dirty white yak poke its head in at the door of the hut in the hope of finding a snack. Nobody felt like moving. I made small talk with the potato lady by the fire; Julie sat in the sun.

J ¶ I need to sit for a while and soak up some warmth and calm down some of the jitters I collected slithering along in the frost. Despite our efforts to joke and pass it off as a gentle afternoon stroll, it was as near to a terrifying experience as I care to come on this trip. There were times when I felt I hardly dared to breathe. But I should not be too concerned, for there have been no premonitions so far. Even when perched on the edge of an icy precipice, my natural instinct for self-preservation intact, I received no hint of those strange calls from within which have become a part of my life since childhood, and which I have come to trust.

Do we all have, I wonder, this mysterious early-warning system, lying dormant, simply waiting to be needed so that it may come to life? When I was nineteen, I dreamed of seeing a city street, with heavy traffic ploughing through a torrential rainstorm. There is no doubt that I *saw* it, visually. The sound of engines was drowned by the swoosh of tyres through the water on the road. Suddenly I saw my brother fidgeting impatiently on the pavement, then dash out into the rainswept street. There was a squeal of brakes and a thud, and he was flying through the air in a shower of glass. The last image before the vision faded was of him lying on his back with blood and rain running down his face into a reddish pool on the ground.

I woke with a clear recollection of the dream and a strange feeling, like a humming, running through my body. All morning the sensation persisted, until I could no longer ignore it. I telephoned my mother, giving her no time to say anything before I burst out, 'What's happened to Clifton?'

She was accustomed to my unexpected questions and un-predictable pronouncements, and didn't bother to ask how I knew. She had just come from the hospital, where they had sewn up his scalp. She detailed the exact events of my dream, adding the only fact I did not know, that it was an ambulance that had hit him.

Such flashes of prescience do not occur when I am looking for them. Yet, after all the cautionary warnings I received from well-meaning friends concerning this Hima-layan escapade, it is hardly surprising if I'm constantly on the alert. Peering into the future, or the present in other locations, or even into the past, is itself a dangerous pre-occupation, a distraction from what is going on around me, and I have no wish to indulge in it carelessly.

Besides, everything out here seems so interesting and fresh – work without mechanisation, villages without traffic. Often the children are very inquisitive, and the dogs are vociferous. If one comes too near, there's a thud and a squeal as an accurately aimed pebble finds its mark. With rabies rife in this part of the world one can't be too careful. Yet it hurts me to hear them yelp. To think that my own dog might ever be treated similarly is unbearable. But it is a world away from the situation with guide dogs. No wonder the Sherpas and villagers were amazed when we showed them pictures of guide dogs being trained. One picture in the book showed a fund-raising walk with guide dogs and owners, and a band of Scots Guards in sporrans and bearskins . . . and everyone shouted 'Yeti!'

My stamina seems to have improved – the 'fifty-yard squeak' is a thing of the past. I just plod on steadily through the day, collapsing without much dignity into my sleeping-bag at the end of it! As I turned in last night, I could still hear the porters telling their friends about the dogs. ¶

Lukla was immersed in grey cloud and drizzling rain, the main street ugly and cheerless, littered with the flotsam that comes from proximity to manufactured goods with plastic wrappers. The airstrip and its tourist trade have attracted entrepreneurs from surrounding villages, from Kathmandu, even from India. Lukla is Khumbu's boom town: new buildings are sprouting up everywhere, traditional Sherpa standing next to modern concrete and corrugated iron. Yet it is big only by Khumbu standards. A moment's comparison to Western towns, and it is just a small village.

A slight figure was plodding up the street, carrying a large bundle of firewood supported by a namlo across his forehead.

'Oh, *Namaste*. Come in!'

Nepal is like that. You have the idea you would like to visit someone, and either you never find them or you just meet them in the street, as if you had arranged it at breakfast.

I sat by the fire in Phurba's little stone cottage, while he warmed the *chang** and looked for some clean cups. Lhakpa had gone to fetch our return flight tickets.

I had known Phurba a long time, since he lived in a remote village at the edge of Solu. No trekkers ever go there – except me – and the life is one of peaceful farming. People have enough to live on, but little cash; and although I loved the quietness, Phurba and his wife had found it too quiet and had moved to Lukla, like so many others, to try their hand at the tourist trade. I had not seen them since their move a year ago.

Phurba's wife was homesick for their farm. 'I miss being near my family. Often in my heart I want to go back to our village – but then I think, no, we must stay and try it a little longer.'

Phurba said, 'It was hard at the beginning. I wanted to run a tea-shop for the tourists, but we have to get some money together before we can start that. Rent is high here, even for this small room. I'm labouring on the site up the hill where they're building a new school. When that finishes, maybe porter work again, I don't know.'

There was nothing to say. The newly-industrialising cities all over Asia are full of families with the same story. Most of

---

**chang* (Tibetan): a local beer.

them will spend their lives trapped in the elusive myth of 'making a start', lured into the glossy trap of consumerism. At least Phurba had come only as far as Lukla. Who was I to try to convert them to the romantic idyll of rural simplicity? To them it is just rural poverty, with no hope of 'making it big', as opposed to urban poverty where there might just be a chance. To appreciate space and quiet you have to have grown sick of urban pollution, of acres of concrete, overcrowding, and the frenetic grab for more wealth – only to find that 'more' doesn't necessarily make you any happier because there will always be something else to want. I sat and warmed my hands at Phurba's fire, the words of a Joni Mitchell song running through my head:

Don't it always seem to go,
You don't know what you've got till it's gone . . .

I could see Phurba's farm: the white-painted stone cottage surrounded by potato fields, a few beans, even some apple trees. The people up there work barefoot in the summer when it's warm.

Lhakpa arrived with the tickets and mail. He and Phurba were soon chattering as if they had known one another for years. The spell was broken; it was time to stop being morose. It is sad to see a culture beginning to disintegrate, especially when it involves your friends, but being gloomy about it is no help to anyone. I braced myself for a return trip down the hillside in the fog, in the dark, with one glass of chang too many behind me.

Out in the street, light seeped through the cracks in the shuttered windows and made auras in the fog. Phurba was standing silhouetted in his doorway, insisting we visit again when we came back to Lukla, and that we bring Julie. Porters had arrived more than two days before with tales of her progress; in the absence of newspapers and telephones, news travels very efficiently around here on simple gossip.

It was an interesting descent: Lhakpa tripped almost as often as I did, but there were no deadly cliffs on the way, so it was hard to take things seriously. I was involved in contemplating the possibilities of guide-bats when we arrived back at camp. I crammed into Julie's tent to read her a letter from home, craning to decipher it by a flickering torch. It had been written in a train, and I kept mis-reading the punctuation. Jangbu mistook the squeals of laughter for squeals of fright and came running over with a torch and a frying-pan to rescue us.

It rained in the night, and I lay awake listening to the drumming on the tent, wondering how much snow was falling higher up and whether Julie could walk in it.

Morning dawned bright and clear with the lightest dusting of snow on the brown slopes above us. It seemed almost inevitable that we would get a serious fall of snow before the end of the trek, but for now at least we had been reprieved. The less time Julie would have to walk in it the better, for she would be sure to find it very tiring.

In the next village we caught up with Lhakpa as he stood chatting with a friend in front of the chörten. The friend was exhorting him to come to his house to drink chang; then he recognised me from a trek out of Pokhara and included us in the invitation as well.

'Nyima Norbu's wife makes really good chang,' said Lhakpa.

What would Solu-Khumbu be without chang? It is indispensable to socialising, hospitality, community co-operation. We accepted.

Nyima Norbu led us through a labyrinth of twisting footpaths between houses and fields to a long row of terraced cottages set at the edge of the village.

'Ooh, the usual ferocious dog growling and barking!'

'It's not that big, actually. And it's got Queen Anne legs.'

'Doesn't sound half so fierce now I know that.'

We ducked into the low doorway and shuffled through the deep leaf-litter of the cowshed. Almost all the Khumbu Sherpas keep their cattle on the ground floor during the cold winter. The shelter keeps the animals alive, and the animal warmth heats the living quarters above. A steep ladder led to a large room where two children were tending a twig fire on an open hearth. Nyima Norbu put on some more wood and a sooty pot of potatoes to boil. The children blew the embers into life.

'*Shea-shea.*' With traditional politeness, Nyima Norbu held out the china bowl of chang with both hands. A dab of butter had been placed on the rim. Julie took it carefully.

'How is this stuff made? No, don't tell me. I'll taste it first.'

She sipped the milky liquid cautiously.

'Oh, it's nice . . . almost like orange juice, and not too sweet.'

'Only made with corn and millet, no rice,' said Nyima Norbu proudly, topping up her cup again.

'I can see with all this shea-sheaing things could easily get out of hand. What does it mean?'

'Eat, or drink, as appropriate . . . just "get it down" really. You'd better slow down, he's just topped up your cup for a third time. Oh, good, now it's Lhakpa's turn. We can watch a Sherpa trying to refuse.'

There followed an elaborate pantomime of refusal and insistence; with, of course, the host being allowed to win in the end.

'How are you going to carry us if you're in no better shape yourself?'

'Don't worry, you just borrow a big enough doko, and I'll carry you easily.'

'You didn't yesterday. You just laughed when I fell over.'

Julie said, 'I want to blow my nose but I daren't put my cup down.'

She need not have worried. Nyima Norbu filled her cup anyway.

Some sprigs of juniper were smouldering in a brazier near us, the scented smoke curling and shining in the thin sunlight filtering through the small window. The rafters were black and shiny with soot. On one of the supporting pillars hung a photograph of the Dalai Lama, draped in a dusty katak. I took Julie on a tour of the room – the carved wooden chest of grain with five heavy woollen blankets piled on top of it, and shelves lining the back wall which held heavy copper pots for water storage and smaller, sooty ones used to boil chang mush, or to cook rice, for party guests. The battered everyday pots were kept by the fire, just plain aluminium dixies such as Jangbu used. There were some more shelves at the far end of the room: these were carved, and on them were displayed rows of brass eating bowls and blue-and-white china cups.

Lhakpa was being shea-shea'd for the tenth time, holding his hand over his cup in protest.

'I can't. I shouldn't. I'm supposed to be working!' His face was flushed, and he was giggling as much as we were.

'You've had it, Lhakpa – drunk in charge of two tourists.'

He tried to prove me wrong by re-packing the rucksack, but it wasn't convincing. Julie sat down and picked up her cup again.

'That's funny, I'm sure it's fuller than it was.'

Nyima Norbu was an attentive host, complementing the chang with a steady supply of boiled potatoes, until Julie began to wonder what she was going to tell Jangbu when she failed to eat his carefully prepared lunch.

The stairs down to the cowshed seemed more difficult on the return journey, as did the narrow, rocky path back to the road. We began to appreciate how well co-ordinated we usually were every time we bumped into each other, or Julie landed on my foot as we negotiated boulders. This latter manoeuvre was guaranteed to cause a crash every time – to everyone's entertainment.

Nyima Norbu took us by a short cut. After fifty yards the path disappeared into a black and evil-looking bog, which had to be crossed by widely spaced stepping-stones. Everyone stopped for a moment, visualising the scenes of chaos this obstacle could cause. Then Nyima Norbu hoisted Julie onto his back and made the crossing in a series of energetic leaps.

Once we were back on the main trail the going was fairly easy, and fortunately devoid of cliffs. After a couple of hours we met a small figure plodding down the road to meet us, kettle in one hand, tin mugs in the other.

'What happen? All the lunch is ready and you are not coming, so I am the search party!'

Jangbu perched the mugs on a convenient boulder and poured the tea. He reminded me of one of my favourite aunties, in manner if not in looks. It had taken a while to get used to being fussed over by someone so small and chirpy. I sometimes wondered if there were any hidden depths beneath Jangbu's sunny and apparently uncomplicated nature, but if there were, he kept them to himself.

It took us an hour to catch up with Dawa at the Alpine Lodge, still trying to keep the lunch warm.

7

Full Moon

The Lodge was a comparatively sophisticated establishment, with a glass bar, formica-topped tables and curtains at the windows. It reminded me of a Midlands transport café. Julie didn't like it. Several similar places have sprouted in the Lukla area as a result of the increased traffic from the airstrip. I preferred the friendly simplicity of the Sherpa houses. The Sherpas thought the place was great. There were even flush lavatories, although they were blocked. Julie took one sniff and refused to go near them.

'I'll wait for the great outdoors, thank you.'

'What, all that rock-climbing through vertical shrubbery?'

'I'll risk it.'

Sure enough, the terrain was steep and uncompromising for the next few miles.

'Don't say I didn't warn you.'

'Brings a new meaning to the word preci-pice!'

'Ugh. Groan of the Day for that one.'

The trail meandered through pine forests and open rocky hillsides, crossing and re-crossing the Dudh Kosi river, which had been so far below us for the last few days. In fact, we had descended very little: the river would have to drop hundreds of feet from where we were now to reach the point at which we had first crossed it below Jubing.

Every few minutes, we would come across lines of porters trudging to the weekly market in Namche Bazar, bowed under their heavy dokos. It seemed that every tea-shop was full of people taking a rest, their baskets lined up on the ledge outside, the Nepalese equivalent of a lorry park. Sometimes a group ahead of us would take a rest in the middle of the road, and almost in unison they would unsling their T-shaped resting sticks, slip them under the base of the doko and lean back, easing off the weight like a forest of tripods. They did not always do it in the most convenient places, and several times Julie and I found ourselves weaving cautiously between tripods, trying not to upset thirty kilos of suntalas poised at shoulder height. If the squeeze became too tight a long whistle would come from one of the porters and the whole 'forest' would uproot itself and move off. It was a strange sensation, having your surroundings suddenly melt away from around you and leave you in an empty space.

Julie's diary recorded a scattering of impressions of the changing scene.

J ¶ Sometimes we walk through the tangy smoke of porters' newly-abandoned fires, the embers so close I can feel the warmth against my legs. There is a constant rustle and patter of bare feet on the road with so many people heading for the market on Saturday. Sometimes I run my hands over a row of dokos parked outside a tea-shop while the porters take a break. Some baskets smell of tangerines, some of onions. Other groups pass reeking of kerosene. The chatter of voices is interspersed with the heavy hooves and tinkling bells of laden yaks and zopkios. They sound so ponderous and majestic, I am looking forward to the time we find one docile enough for me to get my hands on.

Somewhere along the way we were adopted by a little black and white dog; it just trotted along with us and came over to be fussed whenever we stopped to rest. It must be full of fleas, judging by the way it keeps attacking itself, but it is so friendly and so sweet I can't resist playing with it and making a fuss of it. I miss Bruno sometimes. Unfortunately, our new friend changes personality after nightfall and becomes a shrieking, hysterically yapping creature without equal.

We crossed a single-plank bridge with no handrails. The fear it produced in me came from a combination of the disorientating roar of the water, the wobbly plank underfoot, and the apprehension Elaine was transmitting through her hand.

At the bottom of the last hill up to Namche Bazar we walked along the gravel beach of the river itself, with a huge cliff rising above us, echoing the sound of the water until it was all around and above and below us, a great roaring, growling animal full of power.

Having been warned about the awful pull up the hill to Namche I was delighted to find that, though it was steep and very hard work, I made it in the standard two hours! ¶

You could hear the market long before it came into sight. Empty dokos were piled at the side of the road and perched on a huge boulder opposite the market area. Three terraces were crowded with people bargaining, weighing, counting out rupees: Sherpinis with striped aprons and a towel tucked over their glossy pigtails; Tibetans with their pigtails braided up with red wool, cutting a dash in their black coats and felt boots; lowland porters shivering in their thin clothes. Rice, sugar and lentils were being sold straight from sacks in which they had been carried, while biscuits, sweets, woolly pigtails and plastic tea-strainers were spread out on blankets in a splash of colour. A baby yak was trying to eat a cardboard box, without much success. Someone was trying to pick beans out of a sack of sugar. A monk in dark red robes and matching ski jacket was buying Tibetan brick tea.

The meat market was on the top level, although the smell of it extended further. Bloody hides were spread out on the ground, piled with chunks of meat and bone, heads and hooves. The misbehaving bisi would have met its doom here this morning. Hopeful dogs prowled on the fringes, and shiny black ravens flapped overhead, croaking their Nepali name into the mist.

'*Kaak!*'

They flapped out of the way as we approached, glossy feathers fading into the cloud as they found new perches on a nearby rooftop.

Jangbu had made the effort to get here early in case there were bargains to be had. We needed flour, rice and oil – also kerosene, as we were now inside the National Park, where trekking groups are forbidden to burn wood in an effort to halt the drastic deforestation to which this area has been subjected. Two kerosene stoves had been tucked into the bottom of one of the dokos all the way from Kathmandu.

I was relieved Julie was feeling so well, as we were now a little higher than Taksindo Pass, the highest she had ever been. We would go a little higher, then rest and acclimatise for a couple of days before continuing. I told Jangbu to make an early start up to Khumjung so as to have an opportunity to take some photographs before the afternoon cloud blew in and obliterated everything.

Night fell, and the fog froze to hoar-frost on the tents and the white stone walls between the houses and the bare potato fields. Slowly the full moon rose, throwing shadows of the mountains onto the whiteness of the cloudbank, and making the frost sparkle with a cold light. Even the usually pragmatic Sherpas came out to gaze at it in wonder, cold hands tucked into their armpits and their breath steaming in the moonlight. Behind us, Namche Bazar was lit up like a Christmas tree by new electric lights from a small hydro plant in the stream.

I woke to jolly sounds of Jangbu and co. crashing around in the kitchen. My watch had stopped, but the position of the moon didn't seem right for morning.

'Julie, what's the time?'

I knew she could read her braille watch from the warm depths of her sleeping-bag.

'Three o'clock.'

'Good grief, they took this early start a bit literally, didn't they? I suppose they realise we can't go until it's light?'

I could hear a rapid exchange in Sherpa going on in the background. It seemed that Lhakpa was asking the same questions.

'Lhakpa, what on earth is going on?'

'Ah, well, Jangbu doesn't have a watch, and the moon was so bright he thought it was morning and got up and started making tea.'

'Sorry, mistake!' came from Jangbu.

'Is this your idea of a Sherpa joke? Because if it is, you'd better watch out tomorrow when we think of a joke of our own.'

'Pretty good joke, no?'

'Go back to bed.'

Julie said, 'They are daft. They've been at it since twenty to three. I was awake anyway . . . I think I've got altitude problems.'

'What's up?'

'Awful headache. And I feel sick.'

I was concerned that Julie was acclimatising so slowly. It had taken her four days just to get used to being at nine thousand feet, an altitude that bothers very few people. Now, after ten days of trekking at around that altitude, she was ill at eleven and a half thousand feet.

'Breathing okay?'

'Yes, that's okay. And the headache got better once I sat up. So it's probably nothing to worry about.'

'See how you feel in a little while. It gets everyone worse at night.'

We're not going to make it, I thought. No great drama, just a dead kind of disappointment that, after all this effort, and Julie doing so incredibly well on the rough trails, she was not going to acclimatise in the time we had. I wondered how hard it would be for her to give up. A familiar fear surfaced, that sometimes people cover up altitude symptoms rather than go back down, the only safe cure. I felt Julie was quite likely to do this, as she had already been playing down the effect of her cold and keeping up a show of cheerfulness. Perhaps we had time to go a little higher after acclimatising, but it seemed impossible that she would make another six thousand feet of altitude at this rate.

I lay wide awake in the dark hours before dawn, my stomach in a tight knot of anxiety and indecision. Should we go up to Khumjung today or not? Should I confide my present ideas of defeat to Julie? Would it be dangerous to continue to encourage her? High-altitude climbing usually involves pressing on despite mild symptoms of altitude sickness, because of the danger involved in just being on the mountain and the difficulty of carrying enough food to hang around waiting until perfectly acclimatised. Even in large commercial touring groups, half the trekkers experience mild symptoms on the highest day, usually because of tight schedules. It is essential to judge whether the symptoms are merely the early-warning signals, uncomfortable but not harmful in themselves, or something more serious – in fact, deadly if the sufferer does not get down quickly. We had the luxury of dictating our own pace, but we too had a limited schedule.

I was counting days on my fingers in the dark, ticking off how many we would need to make the return journey to Lukla for our flight out. We had only another ten in which to make that extra six thousand feet. It just did not add up. Even so, I knew I was not going to say anything to Julie yet, to help her prepare herself for the inevitable disappointment. I knew that for some stubborn reason I would keep from discouraging her, and would try to watch for danger signs as carefully as I could. We had to keep going as if we were bound to make it. Defeatist talk would only make her worse.

Later, at breakfast, Julie managed some tea and porridge.

'Do you feel like staying here or going on?'

'Oh, let's go on. I'm much better now, and it's dusty here. It hurts my sinuses and makes me cough.'

Another inner debate. We shouldn't go on if she feels ill. But Khumjung is only a couple of hundred feet up this hillside – a quick piggy-back ride down to here or further if she gets any worse. I feel inclined to push things a little while we are so close to the airstrip at Lukla and the hospital at Kunde. Better now than to wait until we are really up in the wilds. It is certainly dusty and unpleasant here.

We pack in the fog and frost.

'Can you post my tape to Rick before we go? It's in a padded envelope, but it's got my mother's address on, so it just needs re-wrapping and re-addressing.'

'Can't we just send it to your mother to post on?'

'No, I don't want to do that. I want to send it direct.'

Being asked to re-wrap parcels without benefit of paper or sticky tape is not what I want to hear at six on a freezing morning in the Everest foothills. I feel like suggesting that people who want to post tapes to their menfolk from the tops of remote mountains ought to come equipped with the wherewithal to do so. Then I manage to restrain myself and we get the thing wrapped in braille paper and posted off. (It didn't arrive.)

The track out of Namche was almost impossibly steep, twisting between boulders and juniper bushes, dividing and rejoining itself in a series of crazy zigzags. We walked slowly, pausing every few minutes to rest. Mingmar and Kaji kept waiting for us, leaning their loads against a boulder, as if they were afraid we would wander off and disappear in the meanderings of the path. Lhakpa finally caught up with us, striding up the hillside, a little breathless. He had a large box of food tied on top of his rucksack.

'Jangbu bought so much food in the bazar yesterday. The Rais couldn't carry it all. They are even having problems carrying what I've left them. And they're feeling the cold. We should take a zopkio from Khumjung.'

I would miss the two chirpy little Rai porters, but I had been concerned about their thin cotton clothes and meagre blankets in this climate.

Julie was already slowing down. The burst of post-breakfast energy and cheerfulness had already run out, and she was gasping for breath every few minutes.

'How far is it now?'

It was the third time she had asked in ten minutes, and I was unable to tell her with any accuracy because the hill was rounded at the top, showing me one false summit after another. I knew it was hard for her, not to be able to see how far she still had to go. In my own experience of feeling exhausted, an endless series of false summits or a thick mist can be most demoralising. Unconsciously you are rationing the little energy you have left: use it all up too soon and you won't make it, but see your goal not too far ahead and a new surge of strength appears within you, as if from nowhere.

'How much further?'

'Sorry, still can't see. Let's have a rest.'

She flopped down into a juniper bush.

'How are you feeling . . . Well, how are you feeling apart from dreadful?'

'Apart from that, not bad! It's like one of those awful nightmares where you're being chased by monsters and are running as hard as you can but not getting anywhere – as if you're running through treacle. It's depressing, that's what it is. Still, the headache hasn't come back, though I do feel a bit queasy.'

There was a ramshackle tea-shop a little further on, and I tried to persuade her to drink some tea.

'Drinking plenty really does help. Being dehydrated will make you feel more queasy.'

She put her tongue into the tea.

'Ugh, it's got sugar in it. Take it away!'

There was nothing here but 'readymix', and Julie wasn't finding the contents of the water-bottle appetising either.

For another slow hour there was little sound but the crunching of gravel underfoot and our own breathing. Ghostly grey trees and rocks appeared silently from the mist, then faded again as the wind stirred the cloud. There was a dank, clammy chill in the air and I wanted to get off this hillside, away from this unfriendly weather and dusty trail, and hide ourselves away somewhere until we were stronger and ready for it. Then it seemed that just as I had given up looking for it, the stone chörten loomed out of the whiteness and we were at the top of the ridge. It was only a few minutes down to Khumjung, where Jangbu would be sure to have the tea boiling.

Julie was suffering severe stomach cramps by the time we reached the camp, but they eased as soon as she sat down and relaxed. She even managed to drink a mug of black tea.

'Maybe it isn't altitude . . . no headache, no breathing problems . . . maybe I might try a bit of this lunch.'

Then she was violently sick.

There was no use making plans or non-plans; she said she felt all right lying quietly in her sleeping-bag. If she got any worse Mingmar and Kaji said they would take turns to carry her down to Namche or even as far as the river. We were definitely not going on until she was drinking properly again. Nausea can be a symptom of altitude, or of dehydration. It can equally be caused by a germ picked up in one of the grubby wayside tea-shops. I gave up tormenting myself about whether or not we had done the right thing to come up here. At least we were camped in a pleasant grassy field.

8

Lhakpa Sherpa

It was a bad night. I thought our canine groupie had abandoned us in favour of the smelly delights of the meat market, but it reappeared halfway up the hill, fluffy tail curled like a banner over its back, looking incredibly self satisfied. It was friendly and well-mannered, and I even saw the Sherpas throw it the odd scrap from the kitchen. Its nocturnal performance was altogether another matter. Even Julie was saying uncomplimentary things about it, and that it was time for it to leave. Poor girl. Just when she desperately needed a good night's sleep the wretched thing had to inflict its neurotic canine ravings on us – and then had the cheek to curl up and sleep peacefully all day! I felt like kicking it myself, just to wake the smug little beast up.

There was no medical crisis in the night. Next morning Julie was fine if she didn't move, and she set herself the task of drinking little and often. Very often.

I wandered over to the kitchen. The Rais were leaving, with shabby bundles of blankets slung over their shoulders, namlos tied conspicuously on top. They would try to pick up another job to take them down from Namche. Jangbu could see I was feeling gloomy, and fed me mugs of salt tea and dollops of Sherpa stew laced with chillies. I must have been getting used to it, for I had a second helping.

I felt restless and at a loose end. I had become totally involved in being with Julie all day, seeing the road as she would feel it, noticing things that would interest her, sometimes perceiving things just as she did, sometimes a little differently. I had become almost an extension of her. More than just a surrogate pair of eyes, I was part of her balance, her moods, a parallel train of thoughts and ideas. It had to be that way or it wouldn't have been safe to come here in the first place. We had to know where the other was moving, what she was thinking. There were too many cliffs and boulders to risk making a mistake. What we didn't know was how we did it. Now Julie was ill and turned in on her own problems and the task of recovering. She needed quiet and rest, by herself, in her tent. Temporarily, I was my own person again. After so many days at such intensity it came as something of a surprise to have time on my hands. What was I going to do with it? Everywhere I walked, I found myself looking behind, feeling I had lost something, wondering why my hand was empty.

Lhakpa said, 'I'm going up to my uncle's house. Do you want to come?'

I followed him through the village. The stone cottages had slate roofs and small square windows; it could almost have been a village in Wales or Scotland but for the prayer flags. Kunde was only a few potato fields above Khumjung, and looked little different except for the clinic with its new tin roof shining in the sun.

Lhakpa's uncle was away working for an expedition; his wife was at home with the children. She bustled us into the best seats by the fire and plied us with tea, chang, and heavy potato pancakes with chilli sauce and melted nak butter. (A nak is a female yak; Sherpas take a perverse delight in asking their clients if they would like to try some yak butter.)

I let them catch up on family gossip for a while, content to warm my hands by the fire and watch the light reflected on the copper pots on the shelves at the back of the room.

Sherpa houses are not cosy. There is usually one big room under the rafters, with an open grate, the smoke finding its own way out. The temperature is often only marginally higher than outside, but the atmosphere is homely, the implements of living very much in evidence – pots, pans, bowls, cups, blankets and stores of food. The only rugs are on benches along the wall. An altar usually stands at the end of the room. The whole family lives, works, eats, sleeps, and prays together in this one room: it seems very natural, very human.

The houses used to have small wood-latticed windows with shutters to conserve precious heat, but since glass came to Khumbu almost all the families have replaced these with larger (though small by Western standards) glass windows. Here the conversion was only just being completed. I once knew an American who lamented the loss of the old windows as indicative that the Sherpas were learning the Western concept of sitting in their houses gazing at the view outside. I had always assumed they wanted the windows to let more light in, so that they could see what they were doing.

I asked Lhakpa's aunt why they were putting in new windows.

'The old ones were small.'

'So why are you having big ones now?'

There was a lot of laughter and she said something in Sherpa that I couldn't catch. Lhakpa translated.

'The old ones were too small to put your head outside. If you did the yetis would get you. Now there are no yetis, so there is no problem.'

I thought it was a suitably Sherpa answer to a Western question and left it at that. As I worked my way through yet another mug of salt tea, I sat back and listened to Lhakpa's cassette of Sherpa songs on my tape-recorder. He had recorded them himself with a portable recorder at a party at his home, and the singing grew more lively and inebriated as the chang flowed.

While we were walking back I said, 'The singing suddenly stopped in the middle of that tape and turned into temple music – horns, cymbals, the lot.'

'No, no. The lamas didn't come to the party! I recorded the *Nyungne** puja at our gompa on the tape before, and it didn't all get wiped off.'

'I thought it was mostly old people who did Nyungne.'

'Not in our village; lots of young Sherpas do it. It's hard: no eating, no drinking, prostrations in the temple all day. But it's a good way to purify bad karma, and I like to go back sometimes. I was studying in the monastery until I was ten.'

'Why did you leave? Didn't you like it?'

'Yes, I liked it, but you know how it is, your friends go off trekking and they come back and tell you all about it . . . so you get curious and you want to go off and try it too. I left because I wanted to go to the Hillary school† to learn English so I could get a job trekking. But my parents wouldn't send me. They were sending Kaji to Hillary school, and I was sup-posed to be in the monastery. For a while I herded our yaks up at the summer pastures. After a few years I was strong enough to work as a porter, and I could earn some money. Eventually I had enough to go to the Hillary school for six months. But you don't learn to write well just going to day school, so after that I worked during the day, and paid the schoolmaster to give me private tuition in his house at night. Then I started working for trekking groups, first just porter work, then kitchen boy. That's the hardest – getting up before dawn in Base Camp in the winter to make the tea for everyone, and you don't have gloves or warm clothes . . . '

I thought of our stoical, uncomplaining Dawa and was glad we had given them warm clothes before we left.

Lhakpa's story surprised me. I had assumed that since his family was wealthy, owning two houses, he had been given a good education and pushed into a relatively good job straight away. Lhakpa went on.

'Some Sirdars are really hard to work for. They are so busy making money they don't care about their staff. Some of them sell off expedition food to hotels – and of course they blame

---

Nyungne (Tibetan): purification.

†Lay schools founded by Sir Edmund Hillary, teaching Nepali, English, and 'Western' subjects.

the cookboy if anyone notices stuff has gone missing. Then it gets taken out of your wages. Or they get you to do extra work one day by saying they'll give you the day off the next day – then of course they don't. Some are really good, and everyone wants to work for them. I went on many expeditions with Ang Dorjee, and he helped me a lot in the early days when I was just nobody. He was the best Sirdar at Ongdi Trekking and he was my friend. He was honest and he didn't cheat and he didn't lie. He's dead now.'

He kicked a stone out of the way and walked in silence for a while, hands thrust into pockets. I saw with sudden painful clarity that Ang Dorjee's death had hurt him as much as it had hurt me, but I knew he couldn't talk about it, any more than I could. He was going beyond words: he was living as he had seen his friend live. Once he had become established as a Sirdar in his own right, with his own responsibilities, he had made some kind of decision about the sort of leader he wanted to be. I knew he wouldn't talk about that either.

I said, 'Do you work for climbing expeditions?'

'Not now. I did before. I climbed quite a lot. It's okay. If you're strong, it's not too hard. It's the only way to get set up with plenty of good equipment: sleeping-bag, down jacket, good pair of boots. No way can a Sherpa buy that kind of stuff out of his wages. You don't usually get any equipment from going trekking, but you need it in Base Camp in the winter. I've got all I need now, and it's easy to get yourself killed climbing mountains . . . trekking's okay, you can drink chang with your friends and have a joke sometimes. Some people keep on climbing and sell their equipment and make a lot of money. It's nice to have a lot of money. But then, you can't spend it if you're dead.'

He took out a cigarette and lit it.

I said, 'That's another good way to kill yourself.'

'I've heard some people say it's dangerous. But doctors in Kathmandu all seem to smoke, so I didn't think there was anything in it.'

'Sometimes I wonder if Asia is the only place left where the cigarette companies are still making huge profits. There isn't much information available out here about what it does to your lungs. People in places like England and America are pretty frightened of it now. Many have given up and a lot more would do so if they could. Even if it doesn't kill you, it makes you weak.'

'When I went climbing I used to stop. Then I'd always start again when we got back to Base Camp!' He looked at the cigarette in his hand. 'That's it then. This is the last one in the packet. When it's gone, I'll do like the English and give them up!'

'I don't suppose you'll find it easy.'

'You'll see!'

We had reached the camp. Jangbu had the eternal pot of tea brewing, and the crew were sitting round warming their hands at the primus stove.

'Julie has drunk half a cup of black tea and half a cup of pineapple juice!' announced the cook, not without some pride.

I stared at the tea-leaves floating around the top of my cup for a while. Then I said quietly to Lhakpa, 'Do you think she is going to get to Base Camp?'

'No.'

I was thinking the same thing myself, but I still wouldn't admit it. Not to Lhakpa, not to Julie, and most of all, not to myself.

'You'll see! We'll get to Base Camp, but you'll start smoking again.'

'No I won't.'

I went over to Julie's tent.

'How's it going?'

'I've been sick again. But the juice stayed down. At least it'll be a quiet night. Kaji said he gave the dog to another trekking group and it went with them to Thangboche.'

I winced as I wondered by what means the dog had been persuaded to leave, but decided to accept the news at face value and to ask no questions.

I had never heard Julie sound so depressed. She had had little to do all day but drink, sleep, and talk to her tape-

recorder. Her thoughts had been heavy, and she said afterwards that she did not want to listen to them again.

J ¶ I kept some juice to drink at night but it froze solid. It's
so cold here. There were avalanches across the valley: a
dull, prolonged rumble, a spine-chilling noise of indomit-
able, relentless power. I hope nobody was in its path.

I feel weak, and so homesick. I would give anything
right now to be back in my own house where I can run
around all the rooms easily, without any help, and I know
where everything is kept. Just to walk down the familiar
streets with Bruno, and make the same old tube journey to
work would be wonderful! I never stopped to think what
it would be like to be on unfamiliar ground for so long
without a break, dependent on someone every time I
want to go anywhere further than the loo tent. Our surroundings are always rough and uneven. I wouldn't dare go
out on my own unless we were in one place long enough
to memorise it and know I was safe – and of course we're
never in one place long enough for that. It's like being in a
cage. The bars are the unknown empty space around me
and the locked door is my fear of it. For me, it's like going
back to a time I would rather forget, when the only way I
could get about was with a white cane. I found it nerve-
racking and exhausting, and I suffered from tension headaches. I became very good at inventing excuses for not
going out at all. Having broken out of that, and having
become independent with a guide dog, it's depressing to
find myself back in that old caged-in state, even though I
know it's only temporary.

Yet, even if I had thought about all this before I came,
it wouldn't have stopped me. You imagine adventures to
be just exciting and romantic fun, and dismiss the idea of
being ill and tired and homesick except in a superficial,
joking sort of way – 'Oh, don't worry about the food, we'll
all have Delhi-belly anyway!'

I have always had a fear of being a burden on people.
I remember the first time it hit me, one day when I was

eleven and was shopping in Newcastle with my mother. I pushed open the heavy glass door of the shop, not realising there was someone on the other side. The door hit a woman in the face as she went to open it. My mother was apologising and explaining that I couldn't see. The woman paused for a moment to say, 'People like you should be drowned at birth' – and then walked off.

I just stood there, trying to take in the implications of what I had just heard, shocked to the very core of my being ... I had never before been made to feel inadequate or inferior, let alone unwanted. An appalling thought struck me. How many other people held the same opinion as this woman? Was I simply being shielded by the love and kindness of my family and friends from the awful cruelty of the rest of the world? My mother did her best to reassure me, but the incident stayed at the back of my mind, making its insidious presence felt at times when I began to doubt myself, eating away at what confidence I had left.

I feel like having a good cry – but I know it would make my sinuses hurt again, so I'd better not. ¶

The next morning dawned crisp and clear, and my photographic conscience was beginning to prick a little. We owed photographs to all the companies that had donated food and equipment, and snapshots-along-the-trail are really not enough; to get a picture worth looking at, everything has to be properly set up. The shapely peak of Tramserku rose above us on the other side of the valley, and in about an hour the sun would come round to the right position.

Julie was feeling a bit better and said she would not mind posing while there was some sunshine, for it might be cold and windy further up. Lhakpa insisted on carrying her up the hillside to our vantage point. Her attempts to refuse assistance fizzled when I pointed out that exertion might bring on the nausea, and then she would get dehydrated all over again.

'But I'm getting off if he starts to collapse.'

'He was telling me this morning how he and his friends go jogging and weight-lifting when they are in Kathmandu.'

'Yes, but this is like jogging and weight-lifting both at the same time!'

Lhakpa made it to the ridge without a rest, trying not to show that he was out of breath.

It was a beautiful situation for photographs: a flat grassy area on the top of the ridge, a few boulders for effect, and some pine trees behind. The valley dropped away in a steep gorge to the east, and on the other side the slopes of Tramserku, steep and forbidding, a glacier-strewn wall of rock and ice and snow, rose to a sharp peak. The Sherpas patiently helped me to set up different arrangements of equipment while Julie rested in the sun until it was time for her to 'star'. She still found that any exertion made her feel queasy, and tried to move slowly and carefully. Jangbu had brought his primus and made pot after pot of tea.

'Now, can you smile and try to look enthusiastic?'

She gave a plastic grin and waved the biscuit in the air.

'There have been days when I could look genuinely enthusiastic about food – but this isn't one of them.'

While she was resting I spent some time showing Lhakpa how to use my cameras. He had used both still and cine cameras before, and was interested in learning more. Gradually, he began to visualise what I was trying to compose, and organised the rest of the crew accordingly. It was reassuring to know that he would be able to take over the photography when I was occupied navigating Julie.

After a few hours the afternoon cloud began to creep up the valley and a chill wind blew damp streamers of mist across our hilltop. It was time to adjourn to the clinic to buy some more cough medicine. Julie walked down to the village, and then felt well enough to continue to Kunde.

As we were crossing a wide, flat field, I let go of her hand and allowed her to walk alone.

'Ooh, are you sure it's safe?'

'Of course I'm sure, or I wouldn't let go. There's flat field in every direction.'

'It's very scary! I've done it before, with people I really trust, but it's very hard.'

'Does one finger make a difference?' I hooked my little finger around hers.

'Oh yes, all the difference in the world. If nothing else, it's a reassurance that if I'm going to fall into a huge hole then the person with me has to be stupid enough to fall in as well! But it's also a point of contact, anchoring you to the world. When you first go blind, you suddenly find yourself in a very empty place. Things just cease to exist when you stop touching them, and you live in this huge cavernous space. You have to learn to keep everything in your mind, even when you're not actually touching it.'

As I thought about this, I realised how much I was anchored to my world by my vision. It told me where I was, which way up I was, where I was going, and, to a certain extent, how I felt about my situation.

Julie said, 'If I don't know what's around me, I make it up – buildings, people in the street, and so on. It's much more interesting than having a blank space all around you. Out here it's a bit different because you always tell me what there is to see.'

Once again, we found ourselves diverted to Lhakpa's aunt's house. The fire had burnt low and she threw a clump of juniper twigs onto the embers. It blazed up, filling the house with sweet, heavy smoke. Julie fled to the steps outside, coughing. When it had cleared, Lhakpa lured us back in with mugs of syrupy-sweet tea. Julie decided she needed the extra sugar.

A friend of Lhakpa's aunt, Lhakpa Khainchi, was offering the services of her zopkio to Base Camp. Her rates were high, and she was asking for food to be provided as well. Lhakpa insisted he was looking for someone who would feed herself and accept the standard rates. He was soon involved in heavy negotiations. I was busy eating potato pancakes. Julie was making a pretence of eating, absorbed in her own thoughts:

J ¶ I'm getting used to the different household sounds: the crackling of the fire with the juniper twigs on it. And I don't need to be told it's juniper, because of the lovely aromatic smell. Lhakpa's aunt is making mashed potatoes to feed her family, rolling the boiled potatoes on a ridged stone – it sounds like an old-fashioned washboard, and the vibrations are transmitted right across the floorboards! One of the girls is making chang, squeezing the mush in her hands so the liquid drains through a strainer into a pot. It makes a 'laundry' sound, like soapsuds being wrung out of clothes, and then the *slap-slap* as she bangs the basketwork strainer against the side of the pot to catch the last drips. Someone is crushing chillies for sauce – a rhythmic thumping of stone pestle in wooden mortar.

I find I cannot stomach those potato pancakes with chilli sauce. I give mine to Elaine, who actually seems to like them, and those unspeakable chillies! I tell her it's just my general lack of appetite and she seems to accept it. Sometimes I wonder why I try so hard to conform, but I suppose by now it's just a habit – constantly trying to conform to a sighted world, so as to be accepted in it and not segregated into 'things for the blind'. I suppose it's one of the main reasons for wanting to be able to make this journey. I have to have a quiet laugh when I catch myself not wanting to admit that I don't like the same food as everyone else!

Even at school (I went to a boarding school for the blind) we prided ourselves on being 'normal', which meant behaving as much like sighted people as possible. I remember two of us taking one of our volunteer drivers on a guided tour of the school on a winter evening – including a rowdy duet rendering of 'Tavern in the Town' on the music-room piano! Our visitor did not seem totally at ease during the tour and remained rather quiet, and somehow non-committal. It was not until months later, when she knew us better, that she told us we had not switched on a single light! At first we were terribly embarrassed – we, who were so proud of our 'sighted' ways! But once we got to the stage where we could enjoy laughing at ourselves, it became one of my favourite jokes. ¶

Lhakpa was counting the hours since his last cigarette.

'Oh Lhakpa, I do feel sorry for you. Have a sweet, or a piece of chocolate or something.'

He took a sweet from the top of the rucksack, and chewed it with evident lack of satisfaction.

'How many do you usually smoke a day?'

'One packet. Twenty cigarettes.'

'How much is one packet?'

'Gaida is only five. But I usually smoke Yak, which is ten rupees.'

'So in one year you've spent 3,650 rupees on cigarettes.'

'My God! So I've been smoking three years, that's . . . '

' . . . That's 10,950 rupees,' added Julie, who was quicker at mental arithmetic than we were.

'Still, you're doing very well not to be getting irritable with everybody.'

Lhakpa was absorbed, working out the things he might have bought with 10,950 rupees.

The hospital at Kunde is traditionally staffed by New Zealand volunteer doctors. Keith and Ellie had been there a year, and would stay for another eighteen months. They had taken a crash course in Nepali, and were popular with the local Sherpas. Ellie was wearing a traditional Sherpini angi, a woollen wrap-over pinafore dress.

'Hello, what can we do for you?'

'Have you got any cough medicine? For a cough like this?' Julie demonstrated graphically.

Keith perused the shelves and handed over a bottle of the same medicine as Julie had just finished. It had been donated by a returning German expedition and no one could read the label, but Julie knew what dose to take anyway.

'And have you got any anti-nausea pills?' Julie explained her symptoms.

'It sounds more like an ordinary stomach bug than altitude — and if it's altitude you should come down anyway.'

'Well, I would of course, if it got worse. Not being able to drink and getting dehydrated just knocks me out completely. And we've *got* to get to Base Camp.'

'Ah, they all say that.'

'Yes, but we're on a sponsored walk to raise money for guide dogs, and my guide dog has made such a big difference to my life, it's something I really feel I want to do.' Julie finished all in a rush.

I saw Keith do a quick double-take: he hadn't realised Julie was blind. Julie sometimes takes a mischievous delight in not letting on until the last minute. I can tell if people know or not by the way they look at her, or, rather, just avoid looking directly at her . . . or, more obvious still, address their remarks to me instead: 'Which bus does she want to get?' and so on. Keith carried it off very well; his voice and his eyes hardly faltered.

'I'll give you a few of these. Don't take more than four a day, and if it persists, come down. You know there's another small clinic at Pheriche? It might be a good idea to drop in and have a chat with the doctor there, an American called Stefan. It's mainly a high-altitude research station, but it's also a clinic for climbers and trekkers – and the Sherpas up there running the hotels . . . No, no – don't give us any money for the medicine. Put it towards the guide dogs. All this stuff is donated anyway! Anything else?'

Lhakpa was leaning in the doorway, forlornly holding two empty fingers to his mouth, inhaling a non-existent cigarette.

I said, 'Not unless you've got any anti-smoking medicine. Lhakpa's having a hard time giving up.'

Keith and Ellie burst out laughing. As I had spoken, Ellie had been taking a packet of nicotine chewing-gum off the shelf and was asking Keith in sign language if she should throw it out.

'Here, you can have it. Good luck! I tried one last week, and it was awful!'

Lhakpa looked dubiously at the packet.

'One piece in place of a cigarette, up to ten pieces per day. In exceptional cases use twenty.'

Ellie said, 'But you're not supposed to get hooked on the chewing-gum. Once you've finished the packet, that's it!'

Lhakpa laughed, and stuffed it in his pocket.

'No problem.'

Keith said we should pay him another visit on the way back; he wanted to know if we would manage to achieve our individual personal goals.

The sky had cleared by the time we got back to the camp. The rock peak of Khumbu Yu Lha above the village was glowing red-gold, the houses at its foot already huddled in shadow. I often wondered why the god of Khumbu had chosen to live on this rock rather than the much grander snow peaks all around. Every mountain has its own god in the Himalayas. For the Sherpa, Mount Everest itself is Chomolongma, mother goddess of the world. A Tibetan friend, Ngawang Tenzing, who had often climbed with Ang Dorjee, once refused the chance to go from the high camp to the summit of Chomolongma, because he did not want to anger the goddess by trampling on her head. A Sherpa called Sundare had gone instead, and had become a successful guide and Sirdar. I doubted if any Sherpa had climbed Khumbu Yu Lha, the protector of Khumbu: no climbing expeditions were interested, and I knew of no Sherpa who would risk his own life and the anger of the god for nothing.

A flock of grey and white snow pigeons rose from a ploughed field in a rush of air.

That night I lay awake listening to the village shaman beating his spirit-calling drum as he walked to the house of an old woman who was sick.

9

Thangboche

It was another bright morning. Dawa came over and told me in a conspiratorial whisper that Julie had eaten nearly all her breakfast.

'What's all this about you feeling better?'

'I feel great! I could write a sonnet about Jangbu's scrambled eggs.'

'I might hold you to that.'

Lhakpa walked over with Tsingdrolma, who ran the little hotel, and in whose field we were camped.

'She says she has zopkio. Sixty rupees a day.'

Tsingdrolma waved her plump hands expansively.

'Very good zopkio. Just like a dog!'

'Does that mean it's faithful or full of fleas?' whispered Julie.

'Actually, I think she might mean the size.'

The zopkios – two of them – had just appeared. They were a sort of Shetland-pony version: most zopkios are as big as yaks but less hairy, and (theoretically) more docile.

Tsingdrolma explained that we would get two for the price of one and that they would carry half the load each.

'And Tawa will come with you to look after them. He'll bring his own food.'

She smiled benignly at the young Sherpa who was en-
deavouring – without much success – to round up the two
mini-zopkios to be ready for loading. Tawa, her nephew, had
come up here to look for work. He was a cheerful lad, with a
turned-up nose and a mop of unruly curls. I wondered how
much experience he had at zopkio-handling as he struggled
to girth up the wooden saddles to which the baggage would
be tied.

Thangboche was not far, and not much higher than Khumjung. We had time before we left to complete yesterday's
photography session, while the sun was right. Tsingdrolma
and Tawa decided to come up the hill to find out what on
earth we were doing on this barren hilltop with two boxes of
food and a tangle of cameras. Lhakpa had to keep moving
them out of the picture whenever I switched to wide-angle.
In the end I decided to include them in the composition
and suggested they should move into the posing group. Both
immediately developed intense stage-fright, and disappeared,
·giggling, behind a boulder.

Lhakpa and Julie sat patiently in front of Tramserku,
supposedly sharing a bar of chocolate.

'Oh, just hang on a minute while this mist clears from the
front of the mountain.'

'Okay!' said Julie, as she whisked a piece of chocolate out
of Lhakpa's hand and popped it into her mouth.

'Opportunist!' I was glad to be able to tease her now she
was feeling better.

The only reply was a self-satisfied munching.

'You definitely get Oink of the Day for that one!'

'Oh, do I? It's so much nicer than not being interested in
food. But I don't want to displace you at the Golden Trough.
Your friends might think I'd done something to make you
lose your appetite.'

Julie was enjoying the feeling of being energetic again, and
on the way down the hill I found her skipping ahead of me,
causing navigational chaos.

'Oops, sorry foot.'

'It's okay. I've got another one. Now watch it here, it goes steep so turn sideways or you'll slip ... *turn sideways!*'

'Sorry, I slipped.'

'You're the one who was underneath. Are you squashed?'

We scrambled to our feet again. Terminal crashes like this were fortunately fairly infrequent, and usually brought on by steep down gradients. If Julie's feet slipped while she was walking behind me, she would inevitably kick me on the back of my ankles, knocking my feet out from under me, where-upon I would fall backwards on top of her.

It would be only a short downhill until the lunch stop at Punkitengma, then a two-hour climb to Thangboche gompa, perched on a narrow ridge above the Dudh Kosi. Tramserku and Kangtaiga seemed to grow larger as we descended, snow-mantled giants towering above us.

'Which mountains do you like best?' Julie asked. 'Do you think of them in climbing terms?'

'No, I don't think so. Not any more. I always used to look at them in terms of approach, danger from hanging ice-cliffs, good lines to climb, and so on. Now I have no interest in going up there, so it just doesn't occur to me to investigate them like that. I suppose if I have anything in mind at all it is how they would compose in a photograph, whether you can get a good foreground, if they're symmetrical or interestingly shaped. From here, Lhotse, one of the highest mountains, is a big, fat, black ridge, but from over in the Arun valley it's a dramatic monolith with sheer black walls. Even Tramserku is changing shape as we walk, turning from an elegant peak to a complex series of ridges and buttresses.'

'It's difficult to get much of a picture of what they all look like,' Julie said, 'and which mountains you can see from different places along the way. I went over that scale model we made, over and over, until I had it memorised, but of course it didn't have all the details of the different shapes of the mountains. Even if it had, I'm not sure I could visualise what part of which mountain would show at a given place.'

'I'm not surprised! It's hard to do that when you're on the spot and can see them. Not only do the mountains seem to change shape, but valleys curve round, and suddenly you find yourself confronted with the other side of the mountain you saw yesterday and were convinced you wouldn't see again.'

'But you still haven't answered me. Which one do you like best?'

'Somehow they're beyond that. I could answer in terms of photography, which is a comparatively superficial way of looking at them. Ama Dablam is beautiful because of the way it sits behind Thangboche monastery; it creates a perfect picture, although it's a bit lop-sided as mountains go – like Chesterfield Church steeple – you know, the crooked spire. Then Pumori, up near Everest itself, is a perfect pyramid of a mountain, standing clear from the ridge. I think its appeal is its simplicity, a child's picture of a mountain – up one side, down the other, pointed at the top, blue sky behind.'

I had been drawing it in the air with Julie's hand, and we both laughed.

She said, 'It's funny but out here you do seem to end up with a more childlike perspective, taking pleasure in simple things, laughing at simple things – '

'Are you trying to make excuses for the standard of your jokes?'

'Look who's talking! Yours are even worse than mine. But you must know what I mean – I'm sure we'll listen to some of our tapes when we get back home and are being "responsible adults" again, and we'll say, "My God, that wasn't us, was it?" And yet it feels so natural.'

'I don't think we're really being irresponsible. We can't afford to be, because the stakes are much higher out here; it's hard and cold and uncomfortable, and there are various degrees of danger depending on what you're doing and where you're doing it. You just cope with situations, and when the pressure's off you relax and joke around. It *is* natural, and that's what I like about it.'

Julie laughed. 'I think the way I cope is by not taking myself too seriously; I try to look at it all like a kid's story or adventure. If it's hard and the trail goes on and on and on and I think "Oh my God, I'll never get to Base Camp – or even camp at the end of the day!" . . . well, I try to get absorbed in all the little things that are going on around me, and before I know it, there we are! Well, usually, anyway.'

'You've exactly described the two kinds of people who come on a guided trek. Some of them become totally immersed in themselves, worrying about their pulse rates and their health and how many people got into camp quicker than they did, or going on about how well they did *last* year . . . Then there are those who just poke around enjoying themselves, taking an interest in everything, rubbernecking at the view, *always* late for lunch! Everyone suffers from sore feet or being tired or ill sooner or later, and it can dominate everything unless you can fix your mind on something positive.'

The conversation had brought us to a tea-shop outside which a group of Tibetans had spread their wares on blankets laid on the ground: bowls, butter-lamps, prayer-wheels, heavy silver jewellery encrusted with coral and turquoise. They called to us in heavily accented English.

'Come and look, very old, I give you good price!'

I began passing things over for Julie to feel.

'She can't see? Tch, tch. *Nyingje.*'

Soon the women were hovering around us, watching fascinated as Julie's fingers 'read' the filigree patterns and carved woodblocks. Salesmanship took second place as they picked out things they thought she would find interesting, no longer caring if it came from a competitor's stall. Julie was handed a tiny pair of cymbals, a brass bowl which hummed when rubbed, and three jingling yak-bells on a leather band. Amidst the ringing and tinkling, she answered questions about her home and her work, how she had learned to read, and of course how she travelled about with Bruno.

'You very lucky come trekking here!'

It didn't occur to these people, any more than to other villagers we had met, to question the value or sanity of Julie's journey. Such doubts had been left behind with the insurance company.

For a long time Julie bargained with the old woman selling yak-bells, Lhakpa acting as intermediary. Julie never liked the Asian tradition of bargaining. She said it made her feel mean, yet at the same time she knew it was expected and did not want to lose face by giving in too soon.

'Tell her I'm not interested any more . . . what? Did she say a hundred and thirty? Sure? Right! Elaine, can you count out some rupees for me? All these notes are the same size.'

As a result, we were late for lunch, in the best tradition of Himalayan philandering. Jangbu no longer seemed concerned.

'No problem. I've kept it all warm.'

While we were leaving, I noticed a small grey cat sitting on a doorstep. Julie became more excited at this news than I had expected, and insisted on going back to stroke it. By the time we had retraced our steps the cat had disappeared. A young Sherpini was standing in the doorway and asked what we were looking for.

'My friend would like to see your cat.'

She invited us into her house and continued with her chores while Julie and I sat on the floor and stroked the cat.

'What I like about going places with you is that you've got the cheek to ask people if I can go feeling over their houses and animals or whatever.'

'Nobody minds. Not in these villages. There isn't such a strong sense of keeping one's personal property private here. There's a long tradition of hospitality among the Sherpas, though it's starting to give way to commercialism in places like Namche and Lukla.'

'I'm really glad we came in the off-season, even if it is cold. People have time to stop and chat. I can't imagine someone coming to my door in London and asking to stroke my cat.'

This valley is one of the few in Khumbu where there is still dead wood available to be collected, and we met groups of youngsters trudging back up the hill with bundles they had gathered in the morning. School had just finished for a two-month break, and during these cold months the children would spend most days collecting firewood. It takes a day to bring home just one bundle.

We caught up with the zopkios grazing idly at the side of the trail. Tawa was nowhere to be seen. Lhakpa looked

18 Tsingdrolma with Julie.

19 Lhakpa, Jangbu and Tawa loading the zopkios.

20 Thangboche monastery, with the mountains of Gokyo behind.

21 Prayer-wheels at Thangboche.

22 Lhotse Shar and a boulder carved with mantras, from above
   Pangboche.
23 Jangbu and Dawa cooking lunch in their open-air kitchen.

24 Julie at the hermitage. The Chukhung valley lies below, with the
mountains of Baruntse and Makalu beyond.

around for a minute, then gave the nearest animal a hearty slap on the rump, urging it back onto the trail again.

'*Sho-sho-woh!*'

After more shouts and piercing whistles the two laden beasts plodded on up the road. Lhakpa followed, controlling them with his voice with an ease and skill that could have come only from long experience. He began to whistle, a wistful, haunting tune that spoke of men alone for long months in the mountains with their animals.

'Zopkio song,' he said, and whistled again, the refrain lifting and swaying, unpredictable as the mountain wind. I wondered what he had thought about during those years he had spent herding his father's yaks up on the high pastures, alone in that expanse of rock and air and light. The song resonated with something familiar within myself, something half-remembered I had felt after spending time alone in the mountains, but could never quite express. It came from the times of not thinking about anything, when you could switch off that constant internal chatter and just *be* – and in the ensuing quietness you could hear the rhythms of air and water as a song.

Grey mist had closed in gently over the hillside, ghosting the trees and rocks and softening the distant roar of the river. Long strands of white-green lichen hung from the trees, wafting ever so slightly with the movement of the damp air. There was an atmosphere of mystery about this place, as if the magical happenings of Sherpa mythology could manifest here, now, even in this age of unbelief.

The road had become an expanse of soft white sand that silenced our footsteps and ran ahead like a white ribbon into the mist. The bearded pine forest gave way to sweet-smelling juniper and rhododendron bushes with their leaves closed, like drooping hands in the cold. Herbs and grasses, their leaves winter-brown and dry, grew close to the ground, a woolly rug between the rocks and bushes. Every boulder was carved with the mantra OM MANI PADME HUM, black letters on a white chiselled background: we were walking across a page of scriptures, a great fold of fossilised prayer flag.

Julie said, 'You know, the further we go, the more of a feeling I get for the mountains, even though I can't see them. Not just their physical presence, but also a sense of my relationship with them, a kind of respect and acknowledgement of what it entails just to be here. The more I put myself into it, the more exertion I make, the closer I feel to actually *being* here.'

I knew exactly what she meant.

'I think you have to give something of yourself to any situation really to experience it, rather than just being a voyeur. Up here everything is intensified somehow. The rewards can be far greater, and so can the cost. I've always felt that the jet-setters who helicopter in to places like the Everest View Hotel, stay a night in their oxygen-supplied rooms, and then airlift out again, are really just fooling themselves. They're not *experiencing* the mountains because they're not experiencing anything of themselves. They've put a barrier around themselves so that it is as if they are watching a giant television screen.'

'Isn't that the difference between being here and city life? You seem to close yourself in in the city, to protect yourself, while here in the mountains – or in any wild area – you have to start letting go and blending with your surroundings.'

'I'm sure you're right,' I said. 'There are the two kinds of people I meet on the trekking groups I've guided. Some will cling tightly to all the affectations and trappings with which they surround themselves in their jobs and social lives and so on . . . and of course it's much harder to do that out here in these conditions, when you're physically tired and under pressure anyway. They often finish up exhausted! But then you see some of them start to let go, becoming open, letting things in, letting things happen. And then you don't need to talk about it – you just look at each other and you *know* you're feeling the same thing and you both just start laughing. I've met people again, years afterwards, who had a terrible time physically, yet still remember the trek as one of the most wonderful experiences of their lives!'

Julie said, 'I don't feel I've experienced a place until I've experienced all its moods, and all my moods too, come to that. You know – you can be in a good mood, and it can be cold and windy and rainy, and it's just exciting! Or you can be in a beautiful place in blazing sunshine when you're in a foul mood and it won't mean a thing.'

We walked on in silence in the mist for a while, then she said, 'This place has the strangest atmosphere about it. I would love to stay here longer. It's one of those magical places where you feel anything is possible. I suppose that's why I've started to think about the things I have . . . things I don't talk about so much, usually because in the practical, down-to-earth world it all seems a bit far-fetched . . . '

'Go on,' I urged, 'Promise I won't laugh.'

'Well, when I was eight I had to go into hospital to have my last eye operation. I went into post-operative shock and was very ill for a while afterwards.

'Out of the blankness of unconsciousness I found myself above the hospital bed I was lying in, looking down at my-self. I began to move away, very easily. I distinctly remember looking down, and seeing a fine, silvery thread connecting "me" with my body on the bed. I don't know how much time was passing, but it was sometimes lighter and sometimes darker, and people came and went. Gradually, I felt as if I was fading away, being drawn down a dark tunnel beyond which was a mass of light so brilliant it dazzled me. Its beauty was more than just its radiance, and although I felt afraid of it, I wanted more than anything to get to the wonderful place I knew was beyond it. Then I heard a voice telling me I mustn't go there, not yet; I must come back to myself. It repeated this over and over again. I wanted to ignore the voice and reach the light – why did it keep telling me to come back? Then the light became dimmer and faded away altogether, and I was back in my body again. But I had a most unchild-like feeling of reluctance and regret that I had not chosen otherwise, that this was the way of heavy burdens and great difficulties.

'When I awoke, the first thing I said to my mother was, "I wanted to go with the angels, but someone told me I had to stay here." My mother told me later that the hospital Sister, who was a devout Catholic and a friend of our family, had sat by my bed the whole time I was unconscious telling me I mustn't leave them, that it wasn't the right time for me to die, that I must come back. I suppose it was her voice I heard. I didn't mention any of it again, because I was afraid people would think I'd made it up.'

There was silence for a while, except for our muffled footfalls in the soft white sand.

I said, 'I've heard of other people experiencing that kind of thing. There was a nurse on a terminal cancer ward who wrote down all the accounts given by patients who had clinically "died" and then been resuscitated. Many of them described something similar. Perhaps doctors should talk to their unconscious patients more often.'

Shadowy figures appeared in the mist.

'Would you like to feel a yak?'

'Oh, wouldn't I just! I can't hear one coming though.'

I stopped the two men who were approaching.

'Excuse me, could my friend feel your yakbi?'

The two Tibetans didn't look particularly surprised. They stopped, and one of them held the baby yak still with one hand on its horn and the other on its curly-haired rump.

'Oh, it's so small! I suppose even yaks have to start small. But it's already got hairy knickerbockers on its legs . . . and its horns! They're such a joke after the terrifying things you've been describing to me . . . these are just like little fat carrots!'

Two monks walking down from the monastery stopped to watch.

'Can't she see at all? Tch, *nyingje* . . . '

'No, she can't see at all. But she can hear, and she can read with her fingers.'

They nodded and smiled, apparently satisfied, and went on their way. For these monks, the greatest tragedy was not to be blind or in any other way handicapped, but to be unable to hear or read the Buddha's teachings; to be unable to understand how to transcend an endless cycle of lifetimes spent trying to satisfy worldly desires.

Thangboche

The entrance gateway to Thangboche is painted with brightly-coloured murals around the inside; mandalas in reds, greens and blues are surrounded by Buddha figures of different colours, each representing a different aspect of enlightened mind. Beyond the gateway the monastery glowed deep red as a stray shaft of sunlight broke through the cloud.

We walked around the building, turning prayer-wheels set on spindles on the side of the walls. Julie was tracing her fingers around the mantras embossed in gold on the wheels, the same mantra as we had found on the rocks on the hillside, but in an older script which I could not read. I smiled as I remembered Tapkhay saying even he found the old script difficult. The wheels were stuffed full of printed sheaves of scriptures; each revolution of the wheel is to release the benefits of the prayer into the air. The whole hilltop was a prayer: it was in the wheels, the rocks, the prayer flags fluttering in the courtyard. We walked without speaking; neither of us wished to break the silence.

From within the monastery a bell sounded.

After an early supper I walked back up to the ridge crest where the monastery stood, and watched the sinking sun flash on the gold spire of the chörten. This place had always fascinated and yet disturbed me; it defied all Western logic and explanation. It was a place of power that was deeper and older than the monastery itself. This was why men had been drawn here to study and meditate in the first place.

I had met the reincarnate Lama of Thangboche the previous year, and he had explained a little of the relationship between men and mountains and gods.

'Each place has its god and the people living there pay attention to it. Khumbu Yu Lha is the god of Khumbu; we do the ceremonies for it which focus the energy of our spirit on the mountain and its god. The power of the god causes the energy in the earth, the fertility and the supply of water, to flow in harmony with the needs of man. There are many different gods, on Chomolongma and Gauri Shanker, on different mountains and in different places. In the practice of Buddha-Dharma, by meditation training, our spirit becomes clear, and clean, and at this point great energy becomes possible for us. It was with this power that the first lamas controlled the gods.'

I came from a technological society which denied the existence of gods on mountains or anywhere else, yet could not provide an alternative explanation for the harmony of natural forces, or why I could feel the energy focussed here. It was not the first time it had occurred to me that to live in a mechanised world of concrete and combustion engines serves to deaden the senses to subtle things which exist outside the sphere of that world. For those who cannot perceive them, such things do not exist. Fair enough really: the secrets of the internal combustion engine have always remained a mystery to me.

I had asked the Lama: 'Are these gods real, or are they just an imputation of men's minds?'

An enigmatic smile. 'All phenomena are imputations of the mind.'

There had been similar moments in conversations with Tapkhay, when time and space would stretch into ungraspable infinity producing an awareness that worlds form, and die, and re-form, while human consciousness could grasp only at its own moment in time. Unable to perceive the true nature of things, we believe that material objects exist in their own right. In fact, according to Buddhist philosophy, all phenomena are merely imputed by mind. Following this train of thought would often cause a kind of inner vertigo, where everything to which I had anchored my ideas would begin to melt and become fluid, and familiar objects would seem less solid. Then I would retreat to my nice comfortable delusions again, knowing they would not satisfy me for long, knowing equally that I would continue to cling to them. Although Buddhism teaches that all things are constantly changing, the hardest part for me is to come to terms with the idea of my own impermanence – that my body, personality and ego will all die, and only my most subtle mind will continue to future existences.

The purpose of the monks' meditation was to clean away

the delusions of the gross mind and become aware of the clear, subtle, innate mind, of which most of us are unaware.

I remembered something Julie had said about trying to describe colours to someone who was born blind: there is no common language with which to describe them. I had the same kind of feeling about perceiving the Buddhist truth. There seemed no point of reference by which ultimate reality could be described in words that could be readily grasped by the ordinary person. Tapkhay always insisted that familiarity with the teachings made the ideas gradually seem less confusing, and emphasised the value of meditation practice in clarifying academic study.

Although it is only the few who will seek the inner realisations of these ideas, the general principle is accepted by lay people as a guide to their way of life. Even the greeting 'Namaste' roughly translates to 'I salute the god within you.'

Lhakpa was walking towards the monastery. The young man with him was wearing red woollen robes, a patched down jacket, and a pair of leather climbing-boots.

'Come in and have tea. This is my friend from Pang Kwam Ma. He's studying here for a few years, then he'll go back to the gompa there.'

I followed through the gateway to the monastery. The heavy wooden door to the kitchen was scored and battered with the passage of pots and kettles to and from the temple. Most pujas are of sufficient duration to warrant regular tea and meals being brought to the monks in the temple itself. The door creaked on its iron hinges, and we stepped through into a world much older than the one we had left outside, with its new airstrips and radios and electric lights.

The walls of the kitchen were soot-blackened, with invitations to all to share fire and food written in tsampa paste, in both Tibetan and Nepali, showing light against the soot. A large stone and clay oven stood at one end of the room; the young monk was stoking it with dry sticks. The huge blackened pots were four times the size of any found in private households, and when full would take at least two men to lift them. Lhakpa's friend blended the salt tea in a tall wooden dongmo, rather like an old-fashioned butter churn. He kept us attentively supplied with tea, while he and Lhakpa caught up on village gossip. I was content to sit and listen, understanding very little of the Sherpa dialect, trying to fathom why being here seemed in a way timeless. It was dark and cold in the large room in spite of the fire, yet I fancied I could hear the jostle and chatter of the monks filling the place at mealtimes. Thangboche Lama had recently left on his annual visit to Kathmandu, and the monastery seemed to rest in utter stillness with only a few monks spending the winter in quiet retreat.

Outside, it was much colder. In the courtyard, lung-ta, the windhorse, whispered in the chill evening air. Behind and beyond, the great wall of Kangtaiga towered above us, grey rock and ice dwarfing us to insignificant specks. It appeared ancient and awe-inspiring, yet itself no more than a fleeting ripple in the passing of time.

The first stars were beginning to shine.

I dreamed I was travelling through a desert country of barren valleys and rocky spires. There was no road and I was scrambling up a mountain of tumbled boulders and terrifying cliffs. Above me was a building: I could not tell from its appearance if it was castle or temple or fortress, but I knew it held within it a secret and powerful knowledge. I wanted that secret, and wanted it enough to be making this unreasonably dangerous journey to reach it. The door was shut. A voice said, 'No. You are not accepted. You cannot pass.' I sat down on the doorstep. It was more than just stubborn persistence because somehow I knew with certainty that there would be no change of mind. There just didn't seem to be anywhere else worth going.

Then, beyond all hope, the door opened and I went in.

10

Pheriche

Morning brought frosted sunshine to Thangboche, and the spring beside the trail was frozen. There were kataks tied to the tree beside the spring as offerings to the naga, the spirit of water. Respect for the naga meant respect for the water. There was a new notice beside the spring. It said, in English, 'Please do not pollute this drinking water with soap'.

We were walking through high-altitude parkland of cropped grass with scattered trees of dwarf pine and juniper. Every boulder was carved edge to edge with black and white letters. The fairytale parkland gave way to dark green rhododendron forest, trailing lichen brushing our faces. Julie was still thinking back to her time in hospital.

'The worst bit for me was having the artificial eyes put in. It's so painful. You have to have them in a bit longer each day to stretch the tissues, which of course have shrunk. They felt like great footballs shoved into my eye-sockets. I was so squeamish about handling them at first. I hated them . . . yet I suppose I'm vain enough to go through it all over again if I had to. I couldn't face the world with my eyelids stitched shut, or whatever it was they used to do to you before they perfected the artificial eye technique. Ooh, your hand's gone all tense! They're all right now. Except when I get dust in them; then they get sore. And I have to make sure I clean it all out, because they don't have a self-cleaning mechanism like the natural eye. The dirt can get right round the back and cause infections, and of course there's a channel directly to your brain – '

'What! How often do you have to clean them?'

'Once or twice a day. I just take them out, and wash them in water . . .'

I walked for a while in stunned silence. Julie volunteered so much about herself it had never occurred to me she had been withholding something as crucial as this during the whole time we had known each other. I had known her eyes were glass, dark brown in imitation of the originals, but she had never said anything about having to take them out and clean them – or about the grim consequences of dirt and infections. We should have been giving her sterilised water every day to ensure there was no risk of infection. Even before we had met up with Jangbu and his kitchen I had made sure she had hot water every day, for a hot-water-bottle because of her cold. I also knew she liked to wash whenever she had the chance. I had simply thought it was because she couldn't see and liked to know she was clean and tidy. It never occurred to me that she was using the water for her eyes.

Jangbu always mixed cold, unboiled water with the washing water. I cursed myself for being so stupid.

'What's the matter? You've gone all quiet.'

'I was just thinking about the haphazard way you've been getting water, and about all the dustbowls we've been camping in. Does boiling sterilise the water enough?'

'It's only been boiled so far and everything seems to be okay – no great lumps of grit in it or anything.'

'Why didn't you tell me?'

'Oh, I just didn't think about it. It's so obvious to me. To be honest, I thought it might freak you out so that you wouldn't want to do the trip.'

'Dead right, it would have! Well, we're here and it's been okay so far, but I think we'd better re-think that idea about crossing the Sahara on camels next year. Deserts are very dusty places, and sometimes there's a bit of a water shortage, you know?'

'Oh, what a shame! I would have loved to do that . . . I've always wanted to.'

There was another long silence, then I said, 'Why are you doing this? Anyone who's been through what you have doesn't need to prove anything, to themselves or to anyone else.'

Julie just laughed.

The path led to a bridge across a narrowing in the gorge; again we were crossing the Dudh Kosi, higher and wilder than before, foaming over rocks and boulders with hardly a trace of turquoise left in the grey-white torrent. Now it was truly the milk river of its name. A cutting wind blew down the gorge, biting through our clothes as we made our way cautiously across the swaying bridge. Beneath the bridge the rocks just above the water were coated in a thick layer of ice.

For a time the trail zig-zagged steeply between vertical cliffs of grey and gold rock, leaving the river further and further below in its bed of white stones.

'Oh. It gets a bit narrow here. Most of the path has just sort of fallen off the rock . . . keep away from the right-hand edge . . . there are no trees to slow you down if you come off here. Turn sideways . . . '

'Sounds like it's straight down to the river.'

'It is.'

There was only a fragile, six-inch-wide band of dirt clinging to the rock slab which fell away below us sheer to the river. The roar of the water echoed up the slab and I hoped it would not upset Julie's balance. It was only for a few yards, but it was by far the worst crossing we had yet encountered. Julie knew from my hand I was tense and was standing completely still, waiting for my signal.

'Okay. Collect yourself and your breathing. Feel ready to go?'

'Yes. Go.'

'Follow me exactly. And keep going sideways.'

We edged carefully across the ribbon of trampled earth. The roaring in my ears grew louder as I concentrated everything on Julie's feet, watching that each step landed exactly on the slender path.

We were across, letting out great lungfuls of air in relief.

'Phee-ew! I forgot to breathe!' Julie collapsed into a juniper bush.

After a while we walked on again and the path was reasonable. I kept crossing that slab again and again in my mind, sometimes as myself and sometimes as Julie. It always came out the same: as Julie, I couldn't do it. As Julie, I could hear the roar of the water and would not trust myself so completely to another person and step blindly out into that awful gap. Julie herself had told me how long it took her to be able to trust someone to that extent, and I'd thought I had understood. Rock-climbing had been like that for me. Trusting someone else with my life, and in turn holding theirs in my hands, had created a bond deeper and closer than any ordinary friendship ever could. Until three years ago . . .

I had been climbing in Derbyshire, trying an overhang I knew was too hard for me. There was no danger; I had a rope above me, and it was fun to try these things sometimes. I fell off under the overhang. Instead of dangling on the rope as I had expected, I fell straight down to the rocks at the foot of the crag and broke my back. Instead of holding the rope, my partner had been trying to retrieve a piece of his equipment. That deep trust had been betrayed, casually and uncaringly, and the shock and disillusionment had left scars deeper than the damaged and painful spine which would always make bending forwards difficult. I realised then that not everyone really understands the subtleties of a finely-tuned relationship; for many it is no more than repeating the appropriate words, but without the true perception that comes from the heart.

Later I went out climbing again, with a different partner. I had got my confidence back, as you are supposed to do, but the only climbs I tackled were well within my standard, rockfaces that I could have soloed. Really, I had been soloing, because as soon as I perceived myself in a situation beyond my control, where once again I had to put my trust in someone else, something deep down refused to let go, refused to take the chance of being betrayed again.

Was this why the bond between Julie and me had formed so quickly? Julie had always understood this kind of trust, and the implicit need for reciprocation of it. She was the kind of friend to whom loyalty was of far greater importance than exchanging pleasantries or being polite all the time. She was the kind of person I knew would never go behind my back, or seek her own interests at my expense. Even here, where the responsibility was ostensibly mine, I knew I could trust her to keep cool on the dangerous sections and do exactly as I directed. If she panicked or did not listen properly, she would be endangering my life as well as her own.

Julie said, 'I want to throw a rock off the edge to see if I can get it in the river.'

'How are you going to do that without throwing yourself off?'

'Will power.'

I looked for a rock or bush on which to anchor myself in case Julie lost her balance, then handed her a pebble.

It fell short of the river, landing in the grass and scrub further down the slope.

'Ah. I enjoyed that!'

'Hmm. Now I hope we don't have to cross this stream.'

Pause.

'Aren't you going to ask why?'

'Okay. Why? Can't you see the bridge?'

'I *can* see the bridge. That's the problem.'

'Nothing for your hands?'

'Not a lot for your feet either.'

'Oh.'

'Not to worry, it's only a couple of feet down to a pair of wet socks if we miss.'

Another side-shuffle on a wobbly plank, and we were across with dry socks and our safety-record intact.

Pangboche is little more than a scattering of stone cottages among a mosaic of small brown potato fields and white stone walls. Tufts of prayer flags sprout from the roofs, and the wooden shingles are held down with rocks whose size testifies to the force of the winter gales.

We walked up the hill to the gompa, set in a sheltered side valley with a little grove of pine trees. Lhakpa disappeared, and came back with the caretaker, an aged Sherpini clutching a heavy key in her wrinkled hand.

'Do you want to see the yeti scalp?'

She led us inside, and up a dark wooden staircase. We entered a large, shadowy room with ornate shelves and cupboards around the walls. There was a small altar in the centre of the back wall. The old woman showed us each of the statues on the shelves, and I asked if Julie could touch them because she could not see. The woman agreed, and I guided Julie's hand over a figure of Guru Rinpoche, smaller than the statue in Junbesi, so that she was able to reach all of it rather than just the feet. But the woman was becoming agitated, thinking we might cause some damage, and for the sake of her peace of mind we reverted to verbal descriptions.

The famous 'yeti scalp' was kept locked in a cupboard in a corner of the room, and this Julie was allowed to touch without causing any alarm. The skull was tall and pointed, with a tuft of reddish hair on top, while the hand bones looked sad and crooked, like those of a deformed child. I thought, if the yeti does exist somewhere up in these mountains, I hope they never find it.

We had intended to camp at Pangboche because it is only three hundred feet higher than Thangboche, but Julie was feeling so lively we decided to go on to Pheriche and spend two nights acclimatising there. Pheriche is at fourteen thousand feet, and it would require another two thousand feet of altitude gain after that to camp at Lobuche.

I said, 'Everything ends in "che" up here! What does it mean in Sherpa?'

Lhakpa laughed. 'It just means "yak grazing place". From Pheriche onwards, people only stay up there in the summer, to herd the yaks – until the tourists started coming and they made hotels. Above Lobuche is also Gorakche, but for some reason all the tourists call it "Gorak Shep".'

'I think that's because it's misspelt on the map everyone uses. It's very difficult to spell Sherpa words in English because the sounds are so different.'

The wind was colder now, whipping up the valley and bringing with it dark clouds heavy with snow. I had not noticed when the view changed, probably because I had been concentrating on the road. This landscape was in stark contrast to the gentle wooded slopes of Thangboche. There were no more trees, only low scrub of thorn and juniper between the dry grass and rocks. The streams on the other side of the valley were frozen, crystalline slivers of solid ice that would not move until spring. Ama Dablam was no longer the attractive background to the monastery; it was a real mountain hung with ice-cliffs. A glacier flowing from its slopes ended in a tumbled grey chaos of pulverised ice and boulders in the valley below us.

Julie said, 'It sounds quite forbidding. But I still feel good, and I'm really loving it! I'm also beginning to feel the distance now. Not technically, but just what it takes to get from Kathmandu to here . . . Kathmandu might as well be at the other end of the world! I know in the first few days I thought, "Goodness, is it all going to be like this?" And it has got harder and steeper, but I've become more able to cope with it. Watching myself adapt to it has been one of the most exciting parts of the whole thing.'

'Strange, isn't it,' I said. 'So many people said to me, "What's the point of Julie going if she can't see any mountains?" and it was hard to explain to them how much more there is to being up here than just looking at the view.

Otherwise everyone would just take a mountain flight and stare out of the pressurised windows for an hour or two.'

'Even reading about it isn't enough; you're sitting there toasting your toes . . . but it's more than just getting cold noses and toeses!'

Conversation ceased for a while as the trail climbed sharply up a low ridge. We had reached the confluence of two rivers and were turning up the left-hand valley to Pheriche. The crest of the ridge was bleak and windswept, a few flakes of snow stinging our faces as we paused to catch our breath.

'Anywhere for a pee?'

'Oh boy, you really choose your moments, don't you?'

'Not even a bush?'

'No self-respecting bush would be seen on this tundra! Hang on, there may be a boulder.'

It was the temperature and velocity of the wind that made the location distinctly unsuitable for the purpose. Julie was remarkably quick about her errand.

'There's rather too much fresh air all at once if you ask me . . . this wind reaches places other winds cannot reach!'

'I got that on tape.'

'Good! I shall play it to my grandchildren as proof of my intrepidness.'

Pheriche lay in a wide valley below us, a low huddle of small houses and a few fields in an expanse of spiky grass and low tussocks of scrub. On all sides were sparsely-vegetated moraines, with the mountains behind half-hidden in the swirling cloud.

We hurried down the slope as the storm increased and crossed the wooden bridge which led to the village. The approach was bordered by low walls of alternate layers of round white rocks and dark slabs of turf — evidence that the village lay on the polished rocks of a huge glacial moraine.

The tents were already pitched in an empty dust-bowl of a field. I looked around but could see nowhere better, and the weather was not conducive to re-locating campsites. What did it matter anyway? It would all be under six inches of snow by morning. Neither of us felt ready for the cold comfort of a wet tent, so we headed for the warmest-looking of the Sherpa hotels.

The room was small, and dimly lit by a single window. Several people were sitting around the fire, cradling mugs of tea in their hands. The atmosphere was warm and steamy, and smelled of cooking, reminiscent of a British chippy. Ang Khandi, the proprietress, emerged from a back room, dusting tsampa flour off her hands and beaming a welcome. Running the hotel had taught her good English.

'Come here, sit by the fire.'

She made the others move up and placed two small stools near the fire.

'Tea?'

She handed us two floury cups, and then went back to preparing the supper.

A tall young American encased in down jacket and trousers clumped through the door clutching a pair of frozen socks. He squeezed into the group by the fire and reclaimed the tea he had left standing on the clay oven. He put the offending socks down on the grubby table in the corner and curled his fingers painfully around the warm mug.

'They just froze to the line! I got my fingers real cold washing them in the river just now. Back in Vermont my folks used to hang out sheets to freeze, then they'd just knock the ice off and they'd be dry.'

He looked ruefully at his reddened fingers. 'I guess socks are not the same as sheets.'

No one commented beyond a few sympathetic nods and grunts. My last sock-washing had been at Khumjung and would have to suffice until we were back there again; the same was probably true for them.

Ang Khandi came back. She had a pressure-cooker in one hand and was wiping flour from the other into her striped apron. People began to drift back to the dormitory next door.

'No, no. You stay.' She pushed Julie and me back into our seats and stoked up the clay oven with sticks and sprigs of juniper.

'People were talking about you. Are you going to Base Camp, Kala Patthar? Is it difficult to walk on our roads? Can't you see anything?'

We fielded the questions separately, and Julie pulled out one of the 'dog-books' to show her. She nodded and clucked her tongue as she turned the pages, then called her two children in to show them too.

'No dogs like that here! Only trekkers. Many trekkers coming here but they never talk about dogs like this.'

'Well, you don't need them if you can see. A lot of trekkers probably don't know much about them. How many trekkers here now?'

'Only six today. Not many. October and April, we're full, no room.'

'Do you like running a hotel?'

'Oh, sometimes it's good, sometimes not. Most trekkers are good people, talking, eating, laughing . . . some are not so good. This morning two people were sitting here, eating breakfast, drinking tea, oh, many cups tea. It's cold, they don't want to go yet. Then time to go they say, "No, only one tea we drink." And they don't pay, shouting, fighting . . . it's no good.'

The Sherpa hotels are all run on a system of trust. You eat and drink freely during your stay, then when you leave you tell the proprietor what you've had and pay accordingly. Inevitably, it was only a matter of time before one or two sharp individuals saw the opportunity to take advantage.

'You staying at Gorakche? My sister Alamou, she's got a hotel there. Maybe you stay with her.'

Somehow it made Gorakche sound like an Alpine resort rather than two makeshift shelters in a wasteland of glacial moraine. We promised to visit Alamou on our way through.

The weather had not improved by the time we made our way back to the tents. Julie disappeared into the loo tent while I struggled with freezing fingers to attach the blue nylon guideline from there to her tent. Julie emerged, grinning.

'If this wind keeps up I think the loo tent's going to be in Lobuche a lot sooner than we are!'

'Give the string a trial run.'

She ran her hand along the string, walking briskly as she always did. I realised, too late, what was going to happen the instant before she tripped over a tent-peg and fell full-length on top of the tent. There was a dull snap which I prayed was breaking tent-pole and not breaking bones. Julie rolled over and sat up.

'What went wrong?'

'The string's too close across the door. I forgot that you usually try it out from the tent, not the other end – so you know what position it's in. Are you okay?'

'I'm fine, but I think the tent's a bit poorly.'

I eased the broken pole out of its sleeve. Lhakpa and Kaji had come over to find out what the commotion was about. I looked at them looking at the pole and remembered I had forgotten to bring the tent-pole repair kit. Making an effort not to lose face, I rummaged about in my pack for dental floss and sticking-plaster – my two all-time repair standbys.

'Now we need to cut one of these angled tent-pegs in half and put a splice each side of the pole.'

Jangbu had just arrived with cups of tea. He looked at the tent-peg appraisingly, assured me it would be 'no problem', and disappeared into the cook shelter. I was still wondering if even Jangbu was in the habit of carrying a hacksaw about with him, when he reappeared brandishing the kitchen knife. The peg was placed on a rock and, after a few mighty chops with the knife, fell apart quite satisfactorily. The Sherpa technique may lack a little in finesse, but it gets things done in no uncertain terms. I spliced the peg to the pole by binding it tightly with dental floss. When my fingers became too numb to continue, Lhakpa and Kaji took over and finished the job. Julie was in her sleeping-bag recording her diary.

'Elaine, where did we stay on Wednesday?'

'When was Wednesday?'

There was still that pervasive feeling that dates and schedules were somehow irrelevant up here; it was only the occasional crisis that provoked a frantic counting of days on the fingers.

My tea was cold, so I walked over to the cook shelter in search of some more. The crew were huddled around the primus stove in a futile attempt to warm their hands. Jangbu still managed a cheerful grin as he heaved the heavy kettle off the flame and poured some tea. The shed was a squalid affair, with wind and snow blowing in through a dozen cracks and holes in the roof, and muddy puddles forming on the floor. Mingmar and Dawa were trying to barricade the open window with a sheet of plastic and an ice-axe, but still the wind came in, and it was bitterly cold. I noticed that Lhakpa had given Kaji and Mingmar his spare warm clothes; I guessed they did not possess enough equipment to be comfortable up here without some help.

I felt sorry for them: because they were working with a 'trekking group', they too were forbidden by law to light a fire while inside the park boundaries. So they sat and shivered around a spluttering primus in their own homeland, while the hotel outside offered hot showers to passing tourists, the water for which was heated every day on a wood fire. Deforestation is a desperate problem in the Khumbu, and there have to be laws and controls, but I felt that somehow the law had got terribly out of balance.

Jangbu was alternating two cooking pots and a pressure-cooker on the stove, enveloping everyone in a cloud of steam as the safety valve released.

'*Oi, sati!** That pressure-cooker's going to explode!' Lhakpa backed away from the hissing cooker.

Jangbu laughed. 'No problem. *Tsup!* Shuttup!' He thumped the lid with his hand and the hissing stopped. 'I did blow a pressure-cooker up once. We were camping down in Jubing with a big trekking group and *baum*! Meat and stew all up in the sky! Next thing, the group leader's down in the kitchen. "Who's dead?" "Nobody's dead", I said. "Just your dinner's spread all over the jungle." So he goes on about safety and insurance and everything. No sense of humour, some people.'

---

*sati (Nepali): friend.

The others laughed. Lhakpa reached for a piece of his chewing-gum and chewed it with evident distaste.

'Ugh, this stuff's terrible.' He spat it out.

'Have a piece of chocolate or a sweet or something.'

'I don't want sweets or chocolate. *I just want a cigarette!*'

He laughed, a little self-consciously, not wanting me to think he was finding it difficult, and rooted around in the stores for a piece of candy.

'The first week's the worst,' said Kaji helpfully.

'And none of us smoke, so it won't be too bad,' added Jangbu.

I looked around the faces lit by the dull glow of the stove and realised we were no longer the group of strangers thrown together by circumstance that we had been only three weeks before. Only Lhakpa and his brother had known each other when we started, and yet already there was a unity of purpose among us. Everyone was trying to help Lhakpa quit cigarettes, just as they were going to do everything they could to help us get to Base Camp to raise money for guide dogs. It was no longer a case of just doing their job: I could tell that from the real delight on Jangbu and Dawa's faces when Julie announced she was well enough to walk on to Pheriche. For them it was a longer walk to a cold and miserable camp, but it was one step nearer to achieving our common goal. As Julie's health had returned, so had the general optimism as to our chances of making it risen.

Jangbu was boiling the drinking water for the following day – a safety precaution against giardia and other 'bugs'. The trick was to get it at night to use as a hot-water-bottle; even Julie admitted she 'wasted' very little on her evening eye-washing.

I handed my bottle to Lhakpa.

'Here, you can have it for five minutes. But then you've got to give it back.'

He tucked the bottle in his jacket and hugged it.

'Hey, this is a good idea. Better than a girl! If more expedition members knew about this, they wouldn't have to take their wives and girlfriends to Base Camp just to keep warm at night!'

'A water-bottle doesn't complain as much either,' added Jangbu.

'Here, you can have your expedition friend back now.' Lhakpa handed me the bottle.

Dawa staggered in and dumped the plastic jerkin of water in the corner. The others moved over to make way for him at the stove, and he held his frozen hands perilously near the flame to thaw them out. I thought of Lhakpa's stories of a cookboy's working conditions and felt guilty that my gloves were better than Dawa's, when he had to fetch the water several times a day. I really only needed my light gloves, for walking with Julie. As I went out I handed Dawa my mitts and was embarrassed by his grin of delight and gratitude. I wondered if it ever occurred to him to feel resentful, or even to complain.

Outside, the wind blew snowflakes into the twilight and a raven perched on the stone wall, black and sinister against the storm.

Somehow I could tell that Julie was lying awake, just as I was, listening to the snow on the tent and wondering how long it would go on, and how we would cope with it. She told me afterwards that our morning's conversation was hovering in her mind, as it was in mine.

J ¶ I wonder why I had never told Elaine about my eyes. Perhaps I should have done before coming on a trip like this. But I just don't mention it to people much. I suppose it's because it relates to a very painful time of my life and I don't enjoy reliving it, although I refuse to let myself hide away from it.

Even before the operation I was already attending a school for the blind and partially sighted, and by the time I was seven my eyes were deteriorating badly. Often I woke up with great curtains of shimmering multi-coloured lights streaming in front of me wherever I looked. I was vaguely uneasy and frightened about this but was scared to tell anybody in case they didn't believe me. So the peculiar optical illusions went on, sometimes increasing in their painful splendour, and then fading away until I almost managed to forget them. The glaucoma and the pressure of fluid on the optic nerves, I learned eventually, was causing them to misfire their electrical stimuli to the brain.

My eyeballs became very swollen and darkly opaque and were permanently bloodshot. My general health was very poor because of the eye condition and I had one childhood sickness after another. Eventually I had to have spectacles with lenses that progressed quickly from lightly tinted to very dark because I could no longer tolerate the light.

I remember the specialist examining me and saying to my mother, 'You know what I have to do, don't you?' But he didn't say what that was. When I had been admitted to hospital before, I had always been told in easy words what the doctor was going to do 'while I was asleep'; this time nobody said anything.

After the first operation I could still see with my right eye but there was a heavy dressing on my left eye which was changed regularly. I spent most of my time lying about feeling miserable, and very much afraid. I was curious to know what had been done to my left eye, but whenever I started to take off the bandage I became very queasy and took my hands away. But at last I forced myself to lift the dressing – and the eye was missing. There was a hollow bordered by the cheekbone, the nose and the eyebrow, and a raw, warm moistness where the eye used to be. I could not believe it, and just sat there by the mirror in a state of shock. I would go to sleep at night convincing myself that in the morning the eye would be there again. When the shock began to wear off I kept telling myself I still had one eye . . .

Just two days before my eighth birthday I returned to hospital. The next day was spent being prepared for the operation. My mother and godmother came to visit me, but the last member of my family I remember seeing was my father. We talked a little, but mostly he just sat and held my hand. When the bell rang for the end of visiting time he showed me the time on his gold wristwatch. Three o'clock. ¶

II

Hermitage

At dawn I could still hear snow brushing against the outside of the tent. There was thick frost on the inside too. I
wondered if Julie felt as unenthusiastic about this acclimatisation walk as I did. I wondered if she was even awake.

'Hey, Elaine, is the weather as awful as it sounds?'

''Orrible. Black clouds coming up the valley, snow, sleet,
wind . . . you name it we're getting it.'

'So what are you laughing at?'

'It's these ravens. You know how they usually look black
and sleek and . . . a bit ominous somehow? Well, there are
about five of them out here feeling the cold a bit, all ruffled up
and undignified and cheesed-off-looking – as if they'd been
caught in their dressing-gowns and slippers!'

'You've got me laughing at them now. I can just see them,
all frumpy and plastic curlers.'

After an hour it stopped snowing and the sun shone between rags of cloud, melting the snow into soggy patches.
Sluggishly, we rearranged our plans for a lethargic day and
began rootling around for frozen boots and gloves.

A huge lateral moraine rose steeply behind our camp. Four
years before I had wandered up this moraine to the rocky
ridge beyond, and discovered a tiny hermitage built onto a

cave perched high on the mountainside. Julie had become fascinated with the idea of visiting such a place, and an acclimatisation walk seemed a reasonable excuse.

As we plodded up the steep slope towards an altitude of fifteen thousand feet, it was hard to believe that Julie had been so ill down at eleven and a half thousand feet in Khumjung. We had come straight up to our present altitude without any rest days until today, and here she was enjoying herself with lots of energy. We were becoming more and more convinced that she had been suffering from a twenty-four hour stomach bug, not altitude at all. If we could reach sixteen thousand feet today, then return to our camp below to sleep, we would be almost sure of having few problems the next day when we would actually be sleeping at sixteen thousand feet, at Lobuche.

Julie was talking about her post-hospital experiences.

'While I was in hospital my mother was trying to visit me and take care of my brothers at the same time. They were both ill in bed with high temperatures. She assumed that the hospital as usual would tell me what was going to happen to me. The people at the hospital assumed that because it was more serious this time, my mother would tell me. So it ended up with nobody telling me I was going to be blind.

'Afterwards, I wondered why I was always led about, and why I bumped into things if I tried to walk by myself. I was convinced I could still see. As I had such a clear memory of what my house was like, and the people in it, and the area round about, I thought I could still really see them. There was also the fact that because the optic nerves had so recently been severed, they were still light-sensitive and transmitting a certain amount of jumbled information to the brain. Even before the operation, while I could still see, those optical illusions had confused my vision. This "phantom vision" is not uncommon with the newly-blinded, but I don't think anyone realised it existed in my case. At first I was weak and disorientated anyway after the operation, and it just took a while to figure out that what I could see didn't correspond with what was there – what I was crashing into.

'It was very hard to give up the phantom vision, for I was left with a terrible emptiness, until I learned to fill it by memorising what was around me. I've learned that other blind people have the same struggle to give up the artificial comfort of the phantom vision – but clinging to it is clinging to the idea you will see again. It takes an effort of will to put such ideas out of your mind. They prevent you from putting any energy into learning the techniques you need to live as a blind person, and so they're very harmful.'

We stopped for a rest and some chocolate at the top of the moraine. Grey clouds were once again blowing up the valley, making the mountains around us appear and disappear like mirages.

'Talk to me. Tell me what you can see.'

'How can I talk to you when I'm eating chocolate?'

'You have a one-track mind.'

On the other side of the valley Ama Dablam stood huge and close, dominating all else around this ridge. The valley below ran north and east and ended in a wall of rock and ice that rose in a seven thousand metre barrier – the watershed between the Dudh Kosi and the great Arun river that flows from Makalu.

We scrambled up the ridge; I had found the hermitage on a similar day of blowing mist, and now had no sure idea of exactly how far it was.

Julie said, 'My legs are starting to feel all treacly again. I wish I hadn't forgotten my water-bottle. I'm really thirsty.'

'The hermitage is above us now. Do you want to go on?'

'I'd still like to see it, if it's not too far.'

The distance was deceptive because it was steeply uphill and the ground was tussocky and uneven. Julie rested after every few steps. By the time we reached the hermitage she had lost all interest in it. She sat on a stone step in a temporary burst of sunshine.

'This is better. I'll just snooze here for a while, I think.'

'You'll be okay going down once you've had a rest.'

I wandered around the cliffs while Julie recovered. There were many caves with rough walls and doors built onto the entrances, the doors now locked and the caves empty. I tried to imagine what it was like to live up here on this freezing mountainside, hauling up water every day, living on salt tea and tsampa cooked over a twig fire and spending the rest of the time in meditation, learning how to escape the round of worldly existence. To me, it seemed that just to be up here was already to have left a great deal of worldly existence behind. The wind blew the cloud in front of the sun, and the ice-hung slopes of Ama Dablam were swallowed up in a blast of stinging cold air. I knew I could not live on this mountain for very long. I was just not tough enough.

Julie was beginning to feel the cold so we set off down towards the camp. By the time we reached the moraine she was stumbling with fatigue and her good mood had gone with her energy.

'I just don't seem to be getting anywhere for all this effort.'

I was alarmed at how suddenly she became exhausted. It seemed far more associated with dehydration than with altitude. We were almost down the hill by the time it became obvious she was feeling ill rather than just tired. The couple of hours without a drink had produced such dire effects that she must have been on the edge of becoming dehydrated the whole time, while I was not even feeling thirsty. I cursed myself for not bringing a spare water-bottle, and asked if she had been drinking all the tea and juice that Jangbu provided.

'But they're such big cups. I couldn't possibly drink it all.'

Jangbu was waiting with the kettle when we reached the camp, and Julie collapsed into bed with a mug, a water-bottle full of juice, and the task of drinking it whether she felt like it or not.

I went to visit the doctor.

The small room behind the door to the clinic was a pleasant surprise: a small wood stove in the centre was producing the first noticeably warm air I had encountered all day. Stefan the American was in his thirties, stocky and bearded, and currently engaged in putting washers onto bolts for attaching sheets of tin to the roof. Two Sherpas were up on the roof, announcing their presence with sporadic but enthusiastic bouts of hammering on the tin already in place. The American trekker and his friend were firmly ensconced by the stove, chatting with the doctor. I wanted to ask him about the effects of dehydration, but it seemed polite to answer their questions first. The trekker wanted to know how we managed to navigate and so on.

Then he said, 'But really, what's the point in her coming, apart from the exercise? Which she could get at home.'

I made a conscious effort to control my impatience. The trekker didn't notice, but Stefan did, and turned away to hide a grin.

'You should ask her,' I said. 'She's having a great time talking to people, seeing things with her hands and so on.' I thought of the dejected figure stumbling down the moraine, and winced at the half-truth – but we had to keep the side up.

'Where is she now?' asked Stefan.

'Over at the camp. I'll go and get her.'

I stood in the soggy field and spoke to the closed tent.

'How are you?'

'Better! Whoopee! I've drunk all but the last two inches of water-bottle.'

'Come on over to the clinic and meet Stefan.'

'Oh, but I'm nice and snug in my sleeping-bag with my tapes, and . . .'

'He's got a wood stove,' I cajoled. 'It's really warm in there . . .'

'How warm?'

'Toasty.'

'If I find you've lured me out on false pretences . . .'

By the time we reached the clinic the two trekkers had gone. Stefan waved us into the seats by the fire and launched into lively conversation with Julie on the audial and tactile delights of Solu-Khumbu. He was the sort of man who showed interest in other people's ideas, and evidently enjoyed listening to a new perspective on his familiar surroundings. Julie had the water-bottle tucked in her jacket, and during the conversation managed to finish off her juice.

'Excuse me bringing my own refreshments, but I got very

dehydrated today and I'm having to drink an awful lot to catch up.'

'How much are you drinking a day?' Stefan asked in his quiet American drawl.

'I'm not sure. Jangbu brings me so much tea and juice, I seem to be drinking far more than at home.'

'We recommend four to six litres a day at these altitudes. You need to take in far more fluid when you're up here. Dehydration makes you far more likely to suffer from the effects of altitude.'

'Four to six *litres*! I'll drown!'

Stefan laughed. 'You can do it! Would you like a guided tour of the clinic in the meantime?'

He took us on the tour, hobbling ahead and leaning on his walking-stick.

'This is the kitchen. You see the hole in the roof above the clay stove? Well, we took the stovepipe out so we could put the new roof on – and I was up on the roof with the Sherpas one day and forgot about the hole. I put my foot straight down it to about the knee and wrenched my ankle. I've been hobbling like this for about three weeks now.'

Outside the kitchen was a solar heating system of which Stefan was inordinately proud – justifiably so, because its efficient simplicity was so well suited to this environment. A length of black plastic pipe, about eight inches in diameter, was supported in a long box with a curved tin reflector behind. A sheet of plastic was stretched over the front.

'It warms up real well during the day. It was a little better before the glass got broken, but the plastic works okay.'

'What broke the glass? Sudden temperature change?'

'No, Sherpa kids I think.'

At the other end of the building was the research section; research was the original purpose for which the Tokyo Medical College had built the clinic. In the middle of a small room was a long cylindrical decompression chamber, an unbelievable piece of high technology in this village of stone cottages and yak pastures.

'Have you had anyone in there yet?'

'Well, no, we haven't, because the instructions are all in Japanese, and nobody here can read them.'

Julie wriggled her way into the metal chamber.

'Potholing expedition next.'

Stefan said, 'There's a phone here to communicate with the outside when you're sealed inside.'

Julie's voice was rather muffled. 'It's like being at work. First phone for over a month!'

There were oxygen cylinders and stethoscopes and a dispensary full of medicinal smells. Outside stood the white fibreglass shed which had been carried up in sections, by porters, for the American Medical Research Expedition in 1981. They had been studying the effects of lack of oxygen on climbers in the expedition, and had brought an extraordinary amount of scientific equipment up to the Everest Base Camp. There has been considerable interest and funding for this kind of research, less because of a desire to save crazy climbers from their own folly than because it relates to heart and lung disease. Researchers found in the climbers superbly fit and healthy guinea-pigs in whom the effects of lack of oxygen could be studied in isolation from the other complications of heart and lung disease, and the findings put together with hospital research.

Stefan said, 'It's real interesting having all these climbers coming through here, not just because of the case-histories of altitude effects, but because they have exciting tales to tell as well.'

We had been drawn back, as if by a magnet, to the room with the wood stove.

'Who's been through recently?'

'There were a couple of British guys and a Canadian on Ama Dablam. They came back here just recently for more fixed rope, then went back up. They had been climbing with Pema, a young Sherpa from Khumjung, but he had been getting repeated dreams of ill-omen, and decided to stay in Base Camp when the others went back up.'

The hammering on the roof finally ceased, and Namka

159

and Ang Rita came in to warm their hands at the stove.

'This is the clinic's maintenance and translation team. Namka also carves mani stones.' Stefan handed Julie the carved stones which had been resting on the shelf behind him. Julie slowly read out the mantra as her fingers traced the shape of the Tibetan letters. Stefan was impressed.

'You can read it? Great! I'm trying to learn, and to speak Sherpa also, but it's hard. Sherpa and Tibetan are similar, but totally different from Nepali.'

'I don't know the whole alphabet, but enough to read these stones if they're clear,' Julie said. 'The bigger ones that are more deeply incised are the easiest to decipher.'

Namka was watching Julie's fingers on the stone and listening intently to what she was saying, but he did not speak, barely acknowledging that the craftsmanship was his.

'There was a party here a while back,' Stefan was saying. Some Americans came through on their way to Everest, and our guys were friendly with the Sherpas who were with them, so you can imagine what happened when we all got together!' He paused for a moment. 'They were really upset afterwards when one of their friends was killed on the mountain.'

'Who was that?' But I already knew the answer.

'Ang Dorjee. I guess he was a pretty popular guy. Namka was crying when he heard.'

'It was only a matter of time with three expeditions a year. Everyone wanted him to go with them, to get them to the top.'

I realised I had spoken with more feeling than intended.

'Was he a friend of yours?'

'Yes.'

'He knew he was going to die. He came in here one evening with Namka saying, "I shall die on the mountain. There is nothing else for me." Maybe he'd had dreams as well.'

I wondered if it had been prophecy or fatalism.

As we walked back, Julie said, 'I went to Ireland for my father-in-law's funeral. They had the service at the graveside and threw some earth into the grave. When the service was over, everyone went away, leaving the grave to be filled in

25 The high valley above Pheriche is encircled by mountains.

26 Khumbu glacier from Kala Patthar. The right-hand fork must be crossed to reach Lobuche.

27 Julie, Elaine and Lhakpa on Kala Patthar, with Everest behind.

28 The way down. Julie gets a 'lift' over a stream.

29 Lobuche again. Julie was still not eating, and an icy wind whipped up clouds of dust, potentially lethal for her eyes.

30 Lhakpa.

31 Kaji and the yak horns.

later. I felt terribly upset; I felt we shouldn't be leaving him there all alone and unprotected.'

I thought of Ang Dorjee lying in the frozen snow of Chomolongma, and shivered.

Dawa had been sent out to tell us supper was ready and we ducked into the cook-hovel for it. Jangbu hovered around Julie with cookpot and ladle, trying to coax her into eating seconds, but although she was eating a little more than before, she did not finish the first plateful.

'Ooh, what was that? Something just ran past.'

'Mouse! It's over there, sitting on the flour sack!' Kaji was stalking it, frying-pan upraised. A few seconds later there was the deafening crash of flying cookpots and utensils.

'What happened?'

'He missed. Well, he missed the mouse. But there are bits of kitchen all over the place. The mouse is probably perched on a kitbag in the corner laughing itself silly.'

Jangbu walked over, holding a water-bottle gingerly by its handle.

'Okay Julie, here's your expedition friend.'

'My what?'

I explained the joke to Julie. She laughed.

'There's going to be a joke about everything by the time we get back.'

I translated. Jangbu and Dawa assured us they would do their best.

Stefan waved goodbye next morning from the roof of the clinic. The sound of hammering followed us up the broad flat valley which ran away ahead of us to the north-west. The rocky spire of Taweche lay before us and to our left, while Ama Dablam was now behind us, silhouetted against the sunrise.

32 Crossing the hilltop below Tramserku. Elaine wondered if she could ever describe it adequately for Julie.

12

Armadillos and Turtles

Lhakpa was walking a little ahead, evidently keeping clear until I was in a better mood. The morning's packing had been slow and frustrating, and I had spent much of the time complaining to him that the camp was too dusty now the sun had dried the surface of the ground; the grit would ruin my cameras. I knew I was just giving vent to feelings of guilt for not having moved the camp myself, not for the sake of my cameras but for concern about the effect on Julie's eyes. Nevertheless, the irritability triumphed and left me still venting my own problems on someone else. Walking in the crisp air and sunshine did wonders to dispel the sourness. Now all I had to do was apologise to Lhakpa.

He was waiting for us at the edge of a frozen river.

'Sorry about this morning.'

'Why sorry?' He grinned. 'I think this river might be difficult. There's water underneath the ice.'

I looked at this latest obstacle in our Himalayan egg-and-spoon race. There was indeed water running beneath the ice – quite a lot of it – and the river was wide. The crossing was obvious, a series of widely spaced stepping-stones which were no more than large rounded pebbles. A slip would mean bruises and rather more than wet feet, and even wet feet were more than an inconvenience in these sub-zero temperatures. Even in the sun, the water was freezing, and wet socks could lead to frostbitten toes.

'No problem!' Lhakpa hoisted Julie onto his back and to my amazement leaped from rock to slippery rock with her. He left her on the far bank and came back for the rucksack. I followed him over a little more cautiously.

The path was no more than a yak-trail through tussocks of spiny plants and the rounded boulders and pebbles of the moraine which lay exposed on the surface. Julie found the going a little easier if she had some advance warning of what size the next area of stones would be, so we graded them into tortoises, armadillos and turtles. Armadillos were the worst, being big enough to trip over but still too small to stand on easily.

'I was talking to some Australian trekkers in Pheriche, and they were coming back from Kala Patthar. It sounds nice. Can we go up there?'

'It's higher than Base Camp.'

'Yes, but it sounds nicer. And what a surprise for those who've sponsored us for dogs – "We went even higher than we said we would!"'

I was dubious. Julie felt fine now, but her sudden attacks of exhaustion worried me. Would it not be better to keep our ambitions to schedule rather than asking for trouble by trying to go higher?

'We'd have to climb up a hill further west than Base Camp. So would you want to go to both places?'

'Well, we could do Kala Patthar first, then afterwards make a trip to Base Camp.'

'You've got it all worked out, haven't you?'

'Oh, yes, if you want an expedition organised, just send for Julie.'

It was a tempting idea. Kala Patthar was a rocky peak eighteen thousand feet high, on a ridge running south from the peak of Pumori. The views from it are superb, and the terrain of tumbled boulders exciting. Everest Base Camp, on the other hand, is a squalid tent city huddled in the shadow of the Khumbu ice-fall, polluted with the garbage of twenty years of Everest expeditions too lazy and uncaring to take out what they brought in.

'We'll see how it goes . . . oops, look out, batch of turtles coming up . . . '

'You know, it is a wonderful feeling of freedom, to be able to change your mind about what you'll do without causing all sorts of trouble, and just to do without what you didn't bring, so to speak.'

'Like a tent-pole repair kit.'

'Mm, yes, I suppose I'll never live that down. What if it had happened in the middle of the night?'

'That would have been very awkward because it's so cold at night our fingers would have stuck to the metal pole while we were fixing it. Even if you escape frostbite when that happens, it can easily tear the skin from your fingers. Speaking of which, your hands are pretty cold. Put your gloves on.'

'Ooh, don't you fuss! It's like having my mother here telling me what to do.'

'Yes, but really, it's probably a good idea to get used to wearing at least thin gloves all the time we're in these temperatures. You could easily touch something metal quite unexpectedly – like a water-bottle for instance – and even if you only got frost-nip it would put your fingers out of commission for quite a while. And you need your fingers more than most of us.'

The sound of harness bells announced the approach of a line of laden yaks carrying supplies up to Base Camp. We moved off the trail to let them pass. I was glad we no longer had the dog with us; on the trail coming up to Namche it always aroused the intense dislike of passing yaks, and then ran to us for protection, pursued by an irate and horn-waving creature of considerable proportions. Julie and I had made several impromptu excursions into the thorn bushes to escape being trampled or simply pushed off the path. According to the Sherpa grapevine, a trekker had somehow fallen off that section of the trail and been killed a few days earlier. This place was quite hazardous enough without bringing extra problems along with you.

Two more frozen rivers and one airy bridge with no handrails brought us to the lunch stop at the foot of the gigantic heap of terminal moraine at the snout of the Khumbu glacier. The two zopkios were grazing the spiky grass between the boulders, while Tawa perched like a gnome on top of a large rock, playing his harmonica. Jangbu made great efforts to create tempting cuisine, convinced that if Julie did not start eating more she would collapse from starvation and exhaustion. Sometimes he would shake his head in perplexity at Julie's incomprehensible biochemistry.

'How does she do it? If *we* miss one or two meals we can't carry loads and we can't keep going. And she eats so little all the time – yet she's still walking.'

There was a shout from Kaji.

'Oi! Tawa! The zopkios have set off on their own.'

Tawa grinned cheerfully, slid down from his rock, and ran off up the slope in search of them. His zopkio handling might leave much to be desired, but his ability to sprint at this altitude was most impressive.

I walked a little way up the slope of the moraine and stood looking back the way we had come. There were mountains all around us: Taweche rose in cold shadows to the south, while Lhotse to the north was obscured by the great heap of moraine above us. The broad, flat Pheriche valley lay behind us now, and beyond it stood Ama Dablam and its surrounding mountains, peak upon peak, ranging away to the east.

Lhakpa had followed me up the slope and was naming the peaks in a rhythmic chant like an incantation.

'Taweche, Lobuche Peak, Lhotse, Ama Dablam, Kangtaiga, Kusum Kanguru, Tramserku, Mera . . . '

The sweep of his arm had come full circle, to the ridge of moraine where we were standing. One spur of the ridge stood out, a little apart, light against the shadow of the valley behind. Along its crest was a long line of small chörtens, each with a tuft of white prayer flags.

'Those chörtens . . . each one is for a Sherpa who died on Chomolongma.'

At the end of the line a new chörten stood a little apart, prayer flags shining white in the sun against the frosty shadows of Taweche behind.

Lhakpa followed my gaze.

'That one is for Ang Dorjee.'

I looked for a while in silence, then turned away down the hill.

'It's too many,' was all I managed to say.

'Yes. Too many. But what to do? It's good money . . . '

Tawa was back with the errant zopkios, and everything was packed ready to move on again. We climbed the steep, crumbly slope of the glacier snout, weaving between huge boulders which had been spewed out of the ice above and had rolled down the slope. Below lay the source of the Dudh Kosi, only a small stream now, under a thick layer of ice.

Julie said, 'It's so quiet here. No birds, no running water, not even any wind since we turned out of the main valley. Can we stop a minute? It's so rare to be able to listen to real silence.'

We sat for a while, until our breathing quietened and the pounding of our hearts slowed. Once we were a part of the silence it seemed to spread out all around us, linking us to the vast emptiness of these mountains. So much of the time we were travelling in a bubble of our own thoughts and chatter, insulated within a small piece of our own world which travelled with us.

We walked on, and the spell was soon broken when Julie tripped over a boulder and landed in an unexpected drift of cold, powdery snow.

'Ooh! That was cold! We seem to have crossed the snow-line.'

'Sorry about that. I wasn't concentrating properly.'

'Today, it doesn't matter. I'm in a good mood and I feel I could take any amount of falling over. It's funny, I tend to have swift changes of mood at the best of times, but up here it's extreme. Sometimes it gets like one of those bad dreams you can't do anything about, and you just have to sit it out and wait until it's over. Does the altitude make you have funny changes of mood?'

'Um, yes – you mean swinging from euphoria to despair and back again?'

'That's me. It's hard enough for me to handle myself when I'm in a "down" mood, let alone anyone else having to cope with me. It's linked with my optimism about whether or not I think I'm going to make it to where I'm supposed to be going. This morning I felt awful. I felt like saying "I've had enough. Can't we just stop here?" And I just stuck it out till it was over, and now I feel great and we're going to get all the way to Lobuche easily, so it must have been mood, not real physical exhaustion.'

I took a deep breath. 'With me, it's mostly frustration at not being able to do the things I know I have to get done. Sometimes it's hard to tell if it is the altitude, or just the fact that everything is so very awkward – you know, wanting to take the tent down but having to put your gloves on so you don't stick to the poles, and your gloves are in your rucksack underneath the cameras, and there's nowhere to put the cameras because there's thick dust all around and you've got to keep them clean ... sometimes I just feel like throwing the whole lot in a heap and saying, "That's it. I don't want anything more to do with any of it." '

We stopped for breath at the top of the ridge. The broad sweep of the Pheriche valley dropped away far beneath us now, and the mountains to the east had disappeared behind the shoulder of rock to our right. Ahead, to the north, a new mountain had come into view – the symmetrical pyramid of Pumori, shining white and gold against a flawless blue sky.

'What does Pumori mean, Lhakpa? As far as I can tell, *pu-mo* means girl, and *ri* means hill – so it should translate as "girl's hill".'

'Mm yes, could be ... ' Lhakpa sounded as if he hadn't thought about it too much.

'Of course, *ri* also means potato in Sherpa, so maybe it means "girl's potato".'

'No! Good joke, but I don't think it means girl's potato.'

He pointed to a pyramid of black rocks in front of Pumori. 'That's Kala Patthar. It means "Black Stone".'

We were walking across frozen rivulets that had leaked out of the glacier during the midday sunshine, ice scrunching under our feet. Sometimes there were patches of snow and the crunching would be replaced by the creaking of the white powder under our boots. Even up here there were occasional patches of spiky, high-altitude grass between the rocks and ice, and some yaks were grazing in the last of the afternoon sunshine. Lhakpa walked towards them, talking softly and holding out a hand towards them. The great beasts lifted their heads to watch the newcomer, and then slowly approached him.

'*Sho, sho* –' Lhakpa kept his hand steady, and one of the yaks nuzzled his palm. In a few minutes he was surrounded by seven of them, snorting softly and stamping their hooves on the frozen ground. They were obviously enjoying the attention. One was having its face scratched, while another was swaying its head back and forth with one of Lhakpa's hands on its horn.

'Would it be safe for Julie to come and have a look?'

'No, I don't think so. Maybe tomorrow we can find one for her.'

The apparent placidness of yaks is deceptive, for they can be temperamental. I have heard of several Sherpas gored or pushed off the road when working with unfamiliar animals. Lhakpa's easy communication was the result of years of experience, and animals can sense this empathy in people very quickly.

Julie said, 'It's like dogs – they can tell at once if someone's used to working with dogs and they respond. It's totally different to just treating them as pets.'

Lhakpa walked back to us with six pairs of bovine eyes following him. The seventh yak was scratching its ear with a back hoof, looking for all the world like an outsize old English sheepdog with horns.

'I think you've worked with yaks before.'

'Oh yes, up on Naulekh, some years. We had five yak, twenty-five nak. But one year there was too much snow, very cold, some died. So we sold the rest. Too much snow in my village.'

Lobuche comprises a few untidy stone hotels in a dusty yak pasture, more closely resembling a group of construction-site outbuildings than a Himalayan village. A large boulder exhorted visitors, in English, 'PLEASE DON'T THROW RUBBISH', in large red letters.

Kaji and Mingmar had just finished putting up the tents in a corner of the yak pasture.

'Sorry for this. We couldn't find anywhere cleaner.'

It was the best of a limited choice; Julie moved in while I checked around for a non-existent better spot, and came full circle back to base.

'Now then, me duck . . . '

'Why are you wearing your Blue String voice?'

I tied the string to Julie's tent-pole, then wriggled inside her tent to formulate a plan of action for the next day.

'So. I think if you're not feeling good tomorrow, but not too bad, we'll wait here and maybe go on the next day. But if you're still feeling as good as this, we could go up to Kala Patthar and sleep down here again. That's the safest, because if you've slept all right here once you should be all right the second time. It does make rather a long day though. Easier stages would be to go up, sleep at Gorakche, and go on the next day, but then, sleeping as high as that is more likely to get you than just walking up there and sleeping back down here.'

Julie thought for a minute before saying anything.

'Three of the trekkers in Pheriche said they weren't affected by the altitude till they slept at Gorakche. But I've not had any problems at night. I'd rather not have to come all the way back here; it sounds much too far to be any fun. I'd rather go up to Kala Patthar and then sleep at Gorakche, and then come back the next day – if I feel okay that is, and I do; I feel magnificent! Couldn't be better.'

Dawa arrived with two bowls of stew, exhorting us to eat it all or we would never make it to Kala Patthar. Julie was almost looking hungry.

'I really think I'm going to eat it all. At sixteen thousand feet too! I'd never have believed it in Khumjung. It is easier to eat since you finally persuaded them we really do prefer stews to fry-ups. Easier to digest. I shall miss Jangbu when I get home – I shall regret all his delicious meals I've sent back uneaten ... I'm sure he would fit into the Red Sausage, wouldn't he?'

'He put it on the other day and went running round the field. There were just two feet sticking out of the bottom. I haven't seen anything like it since I was in Seattle one Halloween. Have you noticed he makes both stew and porridge stiff enough to be able to heap it an inch above the top of the bowl? Must be the only way he can think of to get us to eat more.'

'What on earth is that? Sounds like a yak eating a basket!'

I stuck my head outside the tent door. 'It *is* a yak eating a basket. Be prepared for earthquakes. It's sure to trip over the guy-rope any minute.'

It did. We didn't mind. The good mood had erupted into a kind of euphoric 'rapture of the heights'.

'Wonder if it's anything like rapture of the depths where divers take off their oxygen masks and try to breathe the water?'

'Don't know. But there's not much oxygen up here anyway ...'

'You wait, I'll be in a bad mood tomorrow, feeling terrible, diving into Stefan's pressure chamber – '

'Leaving me running round Pheriche looking for someone who can read Japanese to get you out again.'

'If this is mountain sickness, I can cope. I think.'

'So much for my literary profundity. It's too dark to write now. I wonder if anyone's got a candle? Oh well, another diary entry that just says "see tape". I've done that before,

I'm afraid. Anyway, my pen won't write – the ink's frozen in it . . . "see tape" scrawled in pencil! Wonder if I can read what I've already written . . . no . . . You can't read it with your finger from the other side, can you?'

'No I can't. It's not on that dreadful rice-paper is it?'

'No, it's in a notebook. Didn't you like the rice-paper? It feels nice when you crinkle it.'

'It's very nice for crinkling, but it drove me mad trying to read it. Even my friends were having trouble.'

'I've labelled and numbered your cassettes and put your braille labels inside the boxes. Give me your braille stylus and I'll scratch the boxes . . . can you feel those?'

'Oh yes, so long as my fingers aren't too cold. Where's tape number five?'

'Here.' I handed Julie the cassette.

'No, this is six.'

'I can't see what I'm doing, that's the trouble. This torch is about dead. It *is* dead.'

'Oh, here's five over here. You'd better give me the stylus before I sit on it. Could have dreadful consequences. Oh dear, when I get back people will be wanting to know how many times a day we fell over . . . mostly when I trod on Elaine's foot, actually, and pinned it to the ground.'

'I was doing all right; I was on top usually.'

'You know, I don't think I could explain to someone else how we do navigate. I get a tweak from your hand, and I know if it's not a nervous tweak but a "come over here" tweak, and I just seem to know what to do.'

'It reminds me of learning to ski while towing a sledge. In a tenuous way, it responds to being guided, and if you make a mistake it turns over, or hits a rock, or tangles string round your skis. But a sledge is inanimate – though it's hard to believe sometimes they're not out to get you! When you're guiding a person, there's information coming back at you as you're sending out. I don't think I could analyse it. It's a kind of instinct, and thank goodness it works. I wonder if acrobats or groups of trapeze artists have the same kind of intuitive rapport with each other?'

'That's really why I wouldn't feel safe walking with the Sherpas. Not that I don't trust them, because I feel perfectly safe on Lhakpa's back when he's leaping over rivers with me. It's just that there's no time to build up a finesse of rapport . . . and this is really no place in which to practise. I know I couldn't do it if I'd been led into an accident. In fact, there's only you and perhaps one other person I have that kind of confidence in. If I'd been badly hurt doing something, the way you were, it would have affected me at least as much as it did you.'

'In a way, rock-climbing together made a big difference. To our confidence, I mean.'

'Perhaps it only works because we're friends. When I'm flaked out you don't get ratty and say, "Oh come on, I told you it was a long walk".'

'You'd probably thump me if I did!'

'Well, apart from that, it really makes all the difference getting your verbal encouragement when I can't see the goal we're aiming for.'

'Like when I lie and tell you it's only another half an hour? I know what you mean. Okay, you can't see, but then I can't carry as much as a Sherpa. It's all relative.'

'Obviously it made a difference that you'd been here before and could weigh up if I was likely to be able to cope. For me, the important thing is getting away from the idea that blind people only do "things designed especially for the blind", and are to a large extent segregated from the rest of society.'

'Most people seem to think you're out to prove that blind people can tackle the Himalayas. What they miss is that blind people can be part of a team as much as anyone else; that it's fun for me as well, because we're doing it together. It gives me a totally new perspective on a place which was quite familiar. If we're proving anything at all I think it is that attitude and state of mind are what count in anything. And if what we're doing encourages other people to break down some of those barriers, then it'll have been worth while. All we need now is a windhorse, to spread it around a bit.'

'All we need now is for me to get it together to make it to Kala Patthar tomorrow!'

'In which case a good night's sleep might be an idea.'

I lay awake for a while in my tent listening to the heavy footsteps of the grazing yaks and wondering why, after so much anticipation, it seemed almost unbelievable that we could be on Kala Patthar tomorrow. Maybe . . .

13

Kala Patthar

Morning dawned clear and very cold. Julie was feeling on top of the world – literally as well as metaphorically. So, evidently, were our zopkios, for they had disappeared in the night. Tawa had been out since first light looking for them. Lhakpa lived up to his promise to find a friendly yak for Julie to feel, and I watched with trepidation as she ran her hands through its shaggy hair and along its formidable horns. Lhakpa kept a firm hold of the horns to prevent it waving its head around, and the meeting concluded with zero damage to anything except my nerves.

The sound of a harmonica announced the return of Tawa with zopkios. Lhakpa and Jangbu pounced on the animals and began loading them with the waiting baggage. Julie and I set off ahead, as Lobuche was still in the shadow of the mountains. A little way up ahead was an alluring patch of sunshine. We reached it to find Dawa and Kaji had had the same idea, and joined them on a sunny rock.

Shouts and whistles and the sound of harness-bells from around the corner heralded the arrival of the rest of the team. Dawa and Kaji hoisted their baskets and headed up the moraine. Lhakpa was driving the animals briskly, the haunting refrain of the zopkio song broken by exhortations to *move*. When they reached us, he waved Tawa to take the animals on ahead. Tawa grinned cheerfully, put his harmonica to his lips, and fell into step behind the laden zopkios. Lhakpa watched them go.

'Those zopkios . . . '

The going was easy for a while, along a flat band of spiny grass running between two lateral moraines, but soon we came to the junction where the glacier from Cho Oyu ran into the Khumbu glacier from the west, barring our path. We had to leave the comfortable meadow and climb through the moraine to cross the glacier itself. From the top of the moraine the vast moonscape of the glaciers became visible for the first time, spreading out below us in an expanse of chopped-up white rock and dust, pulverised by the slowly moving ice. Crossing the glacier was hard and unpleasant: there was no proper path because of the constant movement of the rocks, and the ground underfoot was uneven and unstable. As the sun warmed the exposed lumps of grey ice, their surfaces melted, and the rubble perched on top would fall in a series of tiny avalanches.

The sound of heavy yak-bells mingled with that of dripping water and falling pebbles. A long line of yaks approached us, plodding through the chaos of rock and ice. We scrambled to one side to let them pass. They were laden with rucksacks and tents, ice-axes, ski-poles, and the other paraphernalia of a climbing expedition strapped on top. A plump Sherpini was driving them. She waved and called to us as she approached, her gold tooth shining as she grinned broadly at us. It was Lhakpa Khainchi from Khumjung.

'You're doing well! You'll be at Kala Patthar today. I got another job, with my brother. He's Sirdar of this climbing expedition. They're leaving now. Two members died near the summit, so we have to take the equipment out. I think it was the wind. There's a helicopter coming in tomorrow but I don't think they'll find them.'

'Which country are they from?'

'I don't know.' She shrugged. 'We just put their equipment on the yaks. I'd better go now. Good luck!'

She and the yaks disappeared into the glaring whiteness of tumbled boulders.

Lhakpa laughed. 'I'm glad she got another job.'

There was blood on the rocks along the trail; even the yaks must have found it hard going.

Julie said, 'Oh dear. I feel sick again.'

I looked at her sharply. 'Do you want to go back and try again tomorrow?'

'Oh no. It's not that bad, and I couldn't bear having to do all that again.'

'Better take one of those nausea pills to make sure you keep drinking at least.'

'I packed them in the bottom of my kitbag. Which I suppose is miles ahead with the zopkios. I felt so good this morning I didn't think I'd need them.'

'If you can last till Gorakche we can get them out then.'

Why, oh why hadn't I put those pills in the emergency medical kit we always carried with us? It was heartbreaking to think of all the things we had with us, but not the very thing we needed. As before, Julie sank quickly into a state of near-exhaustion, and soon we were moving painfully slowly, with rests every few minutes.

'How much further is it?'

I couldn't tell her. We were surrounded by giant slag-heaps of tumbled boulders and ice. It was impossible to see further than the next mound of debris.

'Listen! It's Tawa's harmonica. We must be nearly at the camp.'

Not quite. Mingmar was plodding back towards us through the tangled mess of rocks and ice, nonchalantly playing Tawa's harmonica.

'You were late coming into camp, so I thought I'd come back to see if Julie needed to be carried.'

I translated for Julie, who was currently slumped over a rock. She shook her head stubbornly.

'I've got to walk it or there's no point.'

'Why not wait here with Mingmar and Lhakpa while I go to camp and get the pills?'

'No, I just want to get there.'

We walked on slowly, as if we had no goal further than the next rock-heap or dusty gulley, on and on in an eternal repetition. If anyone had asked me for an accurate description of hell, I'd have said this came close to the real thing. Nothing lived here; nothing could live in this dry, freezing desert where anything that survived the parched night cold would have the life crushed out of it by the heaving serpent of ice on its inexorable grind downhill. Julie would never make it to Kala Patthar. It was disappointing to be beaten now we were so close. Still, better to have got this far than to have given up down in Khumjung or somewhere. What did those extra five hundred feet matter?

And yet they did matter, and although neither of us could quite explain why, we both knew it was meaningless to try to make excuses and justifications.

We reached the crest of the last moraine, and there below was an expanse of flat white sand with two tiny tents pitched side by side at the edge of it. Within five minutes we were at Gorakche.

Julie went to bed with a cup of water and two nausea pills. I ate a silent and disappointed lunch with the Sherpas. Kala Patthar was a black pyramid above us, mockingly close against a perfect blue sky. I took the cup of black tea from Jangbu and walked over to Julie's tent.

'How are you doing?'

'Not bad, actually,' chirped the tent. 'It went off as soon as I lay down. When are we leaving for the top?'

'It must be dehydration mostly. Make sure you drink all this tea before we go.'

'Mm, don't really want any more. But I'll give it a go.'

Lhakpa looked as surprised as I was when I said we were going. Tawa and Mingmar decided to come too; Mingmar said it was because they had never been up there before, but I guessed they were still concerned about Julie.

We crossed the white sand behind the hut of a 'hotel', searingly bright even through dark glasses, and began the slow plod up the tussocky slope behind. Tawa had brought the zopkios; he thought it would be a nice change for them to graze for a while, as they had been living for the last three days on the hay they had brought strapped in cotton sacks on top of their loads.

As we climbed higher, the full length of the glaciers came into view. The Khumbu glacier ran northward to its source at the foot of the great icefall that spewed out of the Western Cwm of Everest, and southwards from there to the edge of the Pheriche valley, where it melted and dumped its load of rock and dust in the huge moraine we had climbed only yesterday. Had we come up too quickly? Maybe an extra day in Lobuche would have helped, yet Julie had been eating and drinking so little for so long, another day would only make her even weaker. We had left the last and highest blade of thistly grass far behind now, and Julie was slowing down again. The slower we moved, the further away the elusive summit seemed to be, and rests were taken every few steps.

'How far is it now?'

'About the same as we've come from the camp.'

She looked disappointed. I should have lied a bit there. Another few steps, then she stumbled and her knees buckled under her.

'I really can't go on. Won't this do? Isn't this enough?'

I thought, there's no reason why this wouldn't do. She's done so much, suffered so much – isn't this enough? And yet still it wouldn't do. To get so close was a great thing, but to turn away from the goal you set yourself is to give up, wherever you do it. There was no need for Julie to prove her courage to me. But to unite actions with set intentions is a very personal thing that will accept no compromise. It had gone beyond raising money for guide dogs, beyond proving something about blind people; it had simply become something Julie wanted to discover about herself.

'Let's get moving or we'll be late back for tea.'

She staggered to her feet and stumbled on a few more steps, then stopped to breathe again. I looked up at the jumble of black boulders above us. They did not seem to be any closer than they had been half an hour ago. How long would it take at this pace? Another two hours? Another two days? A small voice somewhere inside was pointing out how dangerous it could be to ignore possible altitude symptoms and succumb to summit fever. Yet it was really so close, if only we could move more than a few feet at a time . . . The voice was reciting the list of people who had managed to kill themselves by ignoring their considerable knowledge of altitude sickness and pushing on for the summit. Shouldn't I be persuading Julie to go down?

'This is hell. I just don't feel I'll ever get there.'

'It's really not far now. Do you have a headache, or do your lungs feel wheezy?'

'Both are fine. It's just that I feel totally exhausted.'

I was no stranger myself to the nasty, treacly exhaustion of altitude, and how totally depressing it can be.

'Don't you and the Sherpas ever get this?'

'You bet, but usually a bit higher than this, that's all. It's only because we come up to this height comparatively often that we're getting away with it so far. You'd be the same if you came up here a few times.'

'Ugh! Don't even mention it! If I get off this mountain, I never want to come here again.'

'You won't be saying that when you've done it and you're feeling all pleased about it.'

'I'm not so sure. I really do not feel like moving another step.'

'You'll be furious tomorrow if I persuade you to go back down, now we're so close. Unless you want to go back and give it another try tomorrow?'

'No. There is no way I'm ever going to recoup enough energy to flog all the way up here again. Either I waste the effort I've made so far, or I do it today, though I don't see how.'

Lhakpa said, in English, 'Why not carry to top, take photographs and carry down again? She very tired doing it like this.'

'No', I've got to do it myself or there's no point. It would be cheating. I don't think I've got the energy to explain the finer principles of a sponsored walk just now.'

'I don't think I have either, but it's a delightful example of the way Sherpas view climbing expeditions! Most of them think the climbers just want to be got up there any way they can, just to have their pictures taken on the summit and be famous. And in many cases they're right.'

'Well, not me. I'm going to do it properly. Ugh, I wish I didn't feel so sick.'

I lost count of the rests it took to come within reach of the summit boulders, and even then I was deceived. There was far more scrambling up ledges and outcroppings than I had remembered from my previous visit. Some of the rock-steps were as much as fifteen feet high and were technically difficult enough to make me wonder how on earth Julie managed to concentrate on the moves in her exhausted condition.

'Any other time I would have loved this rock-scrambling, but all I can do is wish it was over. It's just miserable . . . my God, I had no idea it was going to be like this . . . '

I felt like a slave-driver, pushing Julie on when it was obvious she'd had enough. The rules of this strange game we had set ourselves were quite clear: none of us could help her at all, except to encourage her to push herself through more of the same self-inflicted pain. It did little for my self-esteem. I, too, would be glad when it was all over.

I grabbed her hand and hauled her up a vertical rock-step, alarmed at the drop and the jagged rocks below. She surely must feel she was being lured up an inaccessible pinnacle from which there could be no return.

'I think we're there . . . no, sorry, it's a false summit – I couldn't see over the next rock . . . '

'I can't do it.'

'You can, you can . . . '

You bitch, I accused myself. It's not you that's feeling sick.

Then there was a long slender horizontal boulder with a cairn of stones balanced on the cantilevered end that jutted out into space . . . and we were at the summit.

'Here, come and sit on this. We're here.'

Julie burst into tears.

'I don't believe it. I just can't believe it . . . '

'But it is. It is. You did it!'

'I don't believe it . . . all those days and weeks and months. All that effort . . . '

And then we were laughing and crying and hugging each other, and finally Julie did begin to believe it. The great black pyramid of Everest rose across the valley to the east, flanked by the snow slopes of the West Ridge, and Nuptse to the south. An ice-cliff on the side of Nuptse broke off, and the huge slab went crashing down to the glacier with a distant rumble. Everest Base Camp lay far below us, where the ice-fall became glacier. The ridge we were on ran away northwards to the peak of Pumori. There was so much whiteness and glowing gold rock that I was dazzled, and the sky appeared a deep blue around it all, the colour of lapis-lazuli.

'I bet this is the cleanest air you've ever breathed.'

'There isn't very much of it.'

'We're at eighteen thousand feet. There's supposed to be half as much oxygen up here as at sea level. Can you face some photographs?'

'I know, look interested and joyful, and try not to show the vertigo.'

'Now then, it's not that bad, is it?'

'It doesn't feel safe. How are we going to get down?'

'Don't worry about it.' Let *me* worry about it instead. Thank goodness Lhakpa had done most of the photographs on his own, while we were on the way up.

Julie slithered down the rock-steps surprisingly quickly, then sat down again, gasping for breath.

'I wish I didn't get so short of breath.'

'That's a bit like wanting to go swimming without getting wet.'

'I think I'd rather roast on the back of a camel. At least all you have to do is sit there and put up with it.'

'I shall remind you you said that. Look at it this way. If it didn't hurt you'd only want to do something worse tomorrow. Admit it!'

Julie managed a weak laugh, munched the last Dextrosol, and heaved herself to her feet again. Lhakpa insisted on carrying her.

'We get down much quicker this way, and sun's going.'

After a few hundred yards they had to stop again. Julie's stomach cramps had returned and she found it too painful to ride piggy-back.

'I think I'd rather just stagger down slowly under my own steam.'

I had hoped we might travel faster with gravity on our side, but the cramps kept Julie walking cautiously and resting often. It was getting very cold as the sun dropped behind the mountains to the west.

'I have to say I am not enjoying this at all. It's unspeakably bad . . . I've got to rest again.'

'Come on, just keep going a bit, you've done so incredibly well. Don't rest yet, and you can get your own back on me tomorrow.'

'Don't think I'll even have the energy tomorrow.'

The last tussocky slope was taken almost one step at a time. Then we stumbled down into a pool of shadow and onto the white sand.

'We're here. We're on the sand.'

Julie scooped up a handful and trickled it through her fingers.

'It means we're nearly back.'

We walked across the soft whiteness and the sun threw orange and pink rays onto the peaks above us. Nuptse and Pumori glowed softly, no longer rock, but illusions of light against deep purple sky, unreachably, dangerously beautiful. I realised I was crying because Julie would never see them. She squeezed my hand.

'You're as bad as me.'

'I wish you could see this sunset.'

We stumbled over the boulders to the camp and I sat by her tent for a long time while she found dry clothes and got into her sleeping-bag. She was so exhausted I was afraid she would fall asleep before she was insulated for the night.

The mountains around us slowly changed colour from gold to red and purple, to grey and brown, as night came on and the crescent moon rose.

Finally, she slept, leaving me sitting alone in the frosty air, wondering why people needed to climb to the tops of mountains. Even when I had been totally immersed and involved in climbing, I had never really understood why.

14

Loco Doko

I had never seen stars so bright. It did not seem possible that
a few thousand feet could bring them so much closer in this
thin air. Up here they shone with an intensity that lit glacier
and valley with a cold, shadowy light, cold as the ice-cliffs
poised on the cold stone above.

My hands and feet were freezing. I got to my feet stiffly
and plodded over to the hut. The crew were sitting around
Alamou's fire. Nobody was talking much.

I said, 'Do you think we can get a riding yak tomorrow?
We should get Julie down as far and as fast as we can. She's
pretty sick, and it'll take her days to walk it.'

Lhakpa continued to stare at the fire. 'No. Too expensive
for you. Maybe six hundred rupees a day they ask sometimes. We'll do it. We can cut the back out of a doko and
carry her in turns. You should go to bed now and not worry.'

No one else said anything. There was an air of everything
having been decided already. I had been so absorbed with the
events of the day that it was only now I realised it had affected
them in the same way it had me. There was no need to say
anything. It was with a feeling of relief that I went back to my
tent.

It was a cold night. I woke a few times, shivering, and

wondered how the others were surviving. I wondered if Julie was holding her own.

Morning came, bringing light but no heat.

'Julie, how are you doing?'

'No headaches, no wheezes. Didn't sleep well, though. I'm sort of restless and disorientated and can't concentrate. And I'm worried about getting down.'

'They're going to carry you in a doko, so stop worrying.'

Dawa shambled over with some tea.

'Good sleep?'

'Not bad. But how about you three sharing your stuff between five of you?'

'Oh, no problem! . . . Well, little bit cold.'

Knowing Dawa, that was probably an unparalleled understatement.

Lhakpa seemed to have taken charge of the zopkios, and I found him and Jangbu loading the baggage outside the hut. The doko had already been adapted, padded inside with foam mattresses. Dawa returned with Julie's untouched breakfast, concerned because she had eaten nothing since yesterday morning. I hoped we would be able to get past Lobuche to the bottom of the glacier by nightfall, and that the loss of altitude would bring her appetite back.

I brought Julie over to the hut to wait until the others were ready. Even walking a few yards brought the nausea back, and I wondered how on earth she was going to keep drinking today. Alamou offered sugary tea and sympathy, and a place by her fire, away from the biting air outside.

The hotel had been a yak-herders' hut until the expedition route to Everest found it. Now the rough stone walls were lined with wood from packing crates, making shelves for storing canned food sold off by returning climbing expeditions. Pieces of twisted aluminium ladder formed the roof struts; they had probably been used as bridges over crevasses in the ice-fall and were mangled by falling blocks of ice. The hut was roofed over with cardboard boxes covered with layers of old tarpaulin. A homespun blanket hung across the doorway to keep out the cold air.

There was a shout from outside.

'Hey! Watch those zopkios!' Lhakpa stuck his head through the doorway.

'Coming?'

Julie was surprised to find how comfortable the doko was. They had cushioned the basketwork well with mattresses and tied a loop of string to support her feet. Tawa took first turn, so that Lhakpa could get the animals moving. I felt a bit spare with nobody to guide, so I picked up the ruck-sack and followed Tawa up the first moraine. I was surprised how quickly we reached the top. Tawa paused for a brief rest, then continued on into the tumbled chaos of the glacier.

'Hang on a minute, Julie. He's saying you're over to one side and it's affecting the balance. Can you straighten out a bit? Like riding a motorbike.'

'Is that better? I'm amazed he can move at all – I must weigh nearly fifty kilos even though I've probably lost a bit of weight recently. I feel really spoiled.'

'You deserve a bit of spoiling after what you went through yesterday. Make the most of it.'

'I can't believe it's over. I've had this goal fixed in my mind for so long, making me keep at it – and now there's just a space. It will probably be pretty hard to start walking again – and there's not that drive somehow. I can't really describe it; I feel so peculiar physically anyway.'

Lhakpa arrived with the zopkios, insisted on taking the rucksack from me, then ran off up the hill with it to retrieve a wayward animal. Tawa was finally out of breath and stopped to rest with the doko on a flat rock.

'Okay, I'll take it now.'

Lhakpa gave Tawa the rucksack, and slipped the namlo onto his forehead. Then he took off through the tumbled boulders at a pace designed to impress on everyone that he was best at everything, whatever it was. I was impressed – less by the speed than by the fact that he had volunteered to carry in the first place. Most Sirdars, having finally achieved that kind of status in life, would do everything possible to avoid a low-status task such as load-carrying, let alone offer to do it.

'Doesn't he want a rest?' asked Julie, from the doko.

'He says he'd rather have his lunch. Which reminds me, have another Dextrosol.'

'Oh, all right. Or I suppose I'll have to travel all the way to Lukla like this. They must all be tremendously fit. I can't believe we're going so fast.'

'Jangbu was joking this morning that he'd take a turn too, and they all laughed and said he'd be squashed flat in an instant.'

'Oh, poor little Jangbu!'

Then we were coming down the last moraine slope and there was grass below us.

'That's it. We're out of the glacier. Lobuche's just around the corner.'

There was a shout from above us. Lhakpa put Julie down and squinted up the hill to where Tawa was standing.

'Shit. Looks like the zopkios have run off again.'

Casting muttered aspersions in Sherpa on the ancestry of all zopkios, Lhakpa sprinted back up the hill. I pulled Julie out of the depths of the doko.

'My legs feel all wobbly. I ought to be able to walk from here though.'

'Here, let me try what it feels like to sit in. Hey, this isn't bad! Maybe you can walk and I'll take a turn in here.'

By the time Tawa arrived to take his turn, I was nicely ensconced, leaning back, with my feet up on a rock.

'*E, gaa-te* –' Tawa grinned and swore softly, unsure what to do.

'Only joking, Tawa. Don't worry.'

I helped Julie back into the contraption. She seemed to have changed her mind about walking. Lhakpa had caught us up by the time we reached Lobuche. Jangbu was perturbed by the fact that Julie still wouldn't eat, but I fended off his efforts at persuasion, afraid that if she felt any worse she would stop drinking. Even a few steps seemed to bring on the nausea again, and so it was agreed she should ride the distance to the foot of the moraine as well.

'Oi! Tawa! The zopkios are halfway down the valley and we haven't re-loaded them yet.' Jangbu waved his ladle in the direction of the retreating animals.

'These zopkios are a *cheterika* nuisance!' Lhakpa watched Tawa scuttle off after them, then re-organised the team for the afternoon. Kaji and Mingmar would take turns with Julie. We set off, leaving the rest to sort themselves and the kitchen out.

The wind was stronger now, cutting through clothes and whipping up clouds of white dust from the glacier. Every now and then a great blast of grit-laden air would hit us, almost knocking us over and filling our eyes and hair with dust and grit. Julie tried to close her eyes behind her sunglasses as much as she could, but a lot of grit was getting in.

I found myself wincing at every gust, imagining what it must be doing to Julie. I did not want to think about the consequences of an infection while we were still so far from the airstrip. Would the planes be able to fly in this wind?

'I think it'll be okay if I can get all the grit out tonight. Are we nearly down? This wind is pretty unpleasant.'

'It's a while yet, and it's steep. Hang on, Kaji wants to get a drink.'

I steadied the doko while Kaji took a quick side trip to the river.

'Hey, Kaji, do you realise there are yaks standing in that stream further up? Oh, never mind, too late. Here, Julie – more water-bottle and Dextrosol.'

'Oh, all right, just to placate you. Have we passed any other trekkers?'

'Not since Pheriche, in fact. It's really the end of the season. One puff of that freezing Siberian wind and they all head for the beaches in Thailand.'

'I can see their point.'

As if to prove us wrong, two Japanese passed us. They smiled and waved, stared hard at Lhakpa, and walked on.

'You've got them confused. Smart clothes and decked out with cameras – they think you're a Japanese tourist.'

'*Konnichiwa! Arigato!*' mimicked Lhakpa, pointing the camera at us in exaggerated close-up. Then he leaned back against the rock again. 'I think I'll smoke a whole packet of cigarettes when we get back to Namche . . . '

'Oh no! Think of the 3,650 rupees – and the last weeks' efforts wasted.'

Lhakpa looked unconvinced.

'You can't give in now, after we made it to the top.'

'Come on, let's go.'

We reached the valley by mid-afternoon. It was good to have a little more air to breathe. Julie drank some tea, ate two potatoes, and felt pleased. I made encouraging noises, but had hoped she would recover more quickly than this; we were almost down to fourteen thousand feet, far lower than when she had previously felt quite healthy.

Next morning I met Dawa bringing back Julie's untouched breakfast and shaking his head.

'You've got to eat something.'

'I don't like muesli.'

'Well, eat the egg then.'

'It's got cheese in it.'

I went back to the packing wondering why it was taking her so long to recover this time, and knowing that the depression caused by the dehydration would only get worse unless she could begin to drink more.

As soon as we set off I could tell that things were wrong. There was no life in the hand that held mine, and she was tripping over non-existent rocks as we walked. There was no familiar response to signals, while even on Kala Patthar she had been well co-ordinated and alert, in spite of the fatigue. It was as if she had just given up. We would not be able to get across the difficult sections of the trail while she was like this.

'It must be dehydration. Here, have a drink.'

'I don't like this juice. I'd rather have water.'

There was no way we could get water before Pheriche; everything in the water-bottles was juice because Julie had previously preferred it. By the time we reached Pheriche she was exhausted. We sat in the courtyard of the lodge in the company of some Australian trekkers with headaches.

'We're on our way up but we had to stop to acclimatise. What's it like up there?'

'Awful. If I hadn't had a job to do for guide dogs I wouldn't have bothered.'

The words stung. I should never have urged her to keep going if I had known it would make her feel like this. I should never have encouraged her to come here in the first place. And she barely drank half a cup of tea.

We went over to talk to Stefan. Julie put on a remarkable show of being bright and cheerful, and I remembered how she always hated to admit when she was ill. Stefan repeated his advice to drink plenty, but clearly didn't believe she was seriously unwell.

Namka came in with a new mani stone he had carved, a little larger and more deeply incised than the others, just as Julie had said.

'This one is for you.'

He sat with us for a while, going over the script with Julie. He had also carved another, smaller stone with a different mantra, one I did not recognise.

'It's the mantra of Tongden Gelug. It's everywhere around here – didn't you see it?'

I wondered why I had failed to notice it.

Julie seemed to have cheered up by the time we returned to the hotel. She even ate half a bowl of soup, and this encouraged me to give the bad section of the trail a try after all.

In fact, the afternoon went quite well and we made it past the rock slab with less trouble than I would have thought possible. By the time we reached camp in Pangboche, I was convinced Julie had made her usual rapid recovery and would be her old self again in the morning. All she needed was plenty of rest and sleep, plenty to drink. Jangbu had even managed to buy some rice to make rice-porridge in the morning instead of muesli.

The fact that Julie did not eat or drink very much should

have been a warning to me that all was still not well, and morning brought confirmation of this.

'I don't like rice in the mornings.'

'But you've got to eat and drink something.'

'I think if you're really in touch with your body, it tells you what you should and shouldn't eat. And I don't feel like eating that.'

Anxiety was beginning to turn into exasperation; Julie no longer seemed to want to get any better.

'I think it's about time you started to talk back to your body and tell it what's good for it.'

There was an uncomfortable lull in the conversation as we started walking. Rests were frequent, and again there was no response to my hand signals. The anxiety was growing into a gnawing fear that there was something more deeply wrong, something that was not going to be cured by the usual straightforward loss of altitude. We were already low enough to have succeeded by now if that were the case.

'No, I'm not really ill. I think I'm just weak from lack of food.' She prodded her hip bones. 'Gosh, I'm thin. I haven't been this thin since I had anorexia.'

'*Anorexia?* I don't remember you telling me about that.'

'Oh, it was just when I was going through an emotional upset one time.'

Immediately, she was playing it down again. But the mention of anorexia brought a new set of worries piling into my mind. Perhaps this was a kind of anorexia. If so, what was I supposed to do about it? This was not the kind of place to get weak and run-down; the trails were too dangerous and demanding, and it is always at times of waning strength that Asia's indigenous 'bugs' seem to take hold. Already there were signs that the problems were spreading. Julie's foot had become increasingly painful over the last few days as a result of her stumbling and weakness, and this was obviously a contributing cause of her low state. She no longer seemed to want to talk to me, and my attempts at conversation were met by monosyllabic replies, leaving me feeling foolish and useless.

191

I remembered how jolly she had been with Stefan, and also with the Sherpas, in contrast with those negative comments about Kala Patthar and her recent attitude towards me. I came to the conclusion that the trouble lay with me, that she held a deep resentment for the way I had pushed her into keeping going, and that in some complex way she was showing this by being unable to eat and by ignoring me. Part of me wanted to retaliate, to tell her that two could play at being sulky and selfish. I would just leave her until she could be civil and sensible again. This idea died at birth; Julie had no one else here with whom she could communicate, and like it or not I had to stick around and be available if and when she snapped out of it.

But suppose she didn't? She wasn't going to last much longer without food and drink. I had myself experienced the insidious depression and alienation that dehydration can cause, and was still largely convinced that if she would force herself to drink – lots – for about a day, then the depression would cease. What I could not understand was how it had got to the point where she would not even *try* to drink more than a tiny amount. This had not happened in my own ex-perience of dehydration. Perhaps, having failed in her efforts to keep up a cheerful show of being able to cope, she had just given up trying. But what was the solution?

Jangbu and Dawa were evidently concerned as well. Long before we reached Thangboche they met us on the road with tea and soup in carefully-wrapped dixies. Dawa was hovering round Julie, trying to persuade her to eat 'just a little bit' more. It was nice to see her smile again, so I kept out of the way.

A raven perched on the end of a mossy branch, black and glossy against the mountains behind. I took out my camera for a photo – and the raven flew off. Something inside the camera case caught my eye.

'That's funny. What's all this sugar doing in my camera case?'

Lhakpa leaned over, stuck his finger in the white powder and tasted it. In that moment, I realised that the packet of silica gel used to absorb moisture from the camera had burst in the case.

'Hey, Lhakpa! It's silica – poison! Spit it out!'

'Doesn't taste like sugar.'

'It isn't. It's silica – did you swallow any?'

'Not much. Is it that bad?'

'Well, you're not supposed to eat it.'

'Oh well, maybe I'll be dead tomorrow.' He grinned and shrugged, and began to pack up, ready to move on. I wondered if he ever took anything seriously.

That evening, Lhakpa drank four litres of water and started to vomit. I sat with him long into the night, wondering what was the antidote for silica, how long it would take to reach Kunde hospital, and how we would get him there. What would I do about Julie if I had to take Lhakpa to hospital? Suddenly I felt isolated and alone, and very painfully aware that there was no one to turn to for advice or support. I had never worried on the few occasions I had been ill out here: I had felt so physically dreadful I had been past caring what happened to me. To be responsible for someone else who was ill – or worse still, for two people – that involved making difficult decisions. And making the right ones. In the middle of the night with a gale blowing outside.

'Hey, *diddi*. I'll be okay. You're getting cold. You go to bed now.' Lhakpa's face crumpled and he doubled over with the pain again.

After a few hours it seemed that the worst was over and I left him to go back to my tent and try to sleep.

It was a night of alternating stillness and devastating gusts of wind. The pegs kept pulling out of the gravelly earth, leaving the tent flapping noisily in the gale.

The next morning Lhakpa was on his feet again, although he still looked pale and shaky. We had intended to spend an extra day here in any case, and I was thankful for the respite.

It was to be a morning of domestic chores, re-anchoring the crippled tents and re-splicing the broken pole. Then some much-needed laundry, and a foray to the little hotel to buy expedition-surplus canned fruit. It was all Julie had been able to eat the previous evening. At £3 for a small tin, the price was outrageous, even by English standards, but I did not feel in a position to be choosy. Julie was still not speaking to me. I went over to her tent a couple of times to collect her laundry and to ask if she liked mango juice, but her replies were tight and morose, and I retreated quickly.

I spent the afternoon learning Sherpa songs with Lhakpa and Kaji, intrigued by the difficult changing of the rhythm and the subtle complexities of tune. Like the zopkio song, the music seems so much a part of the wildness of the mountains here, where everything has to learn to live in harmony with the seasons and their storms and floods, and the times of respite between.

Tawa was leaving. We had used up nearly all our food, and no longer needed the zopkios. He would take them back to Khumjung and look for another job. There was a bit of quick trading before he left: he had bought a pair of carved yak horns from a farmer in Pangboche and managed to re-sell them to Lhakpa.

Lhakpa was pleased. 'I'll give them to Ongdi as a present. We can hang them up in the office in Kathmandu.'

I looked at the carving. It was the mantra of Tongden Gelug. Namka was right; it was everywhere around here. Now that my eyes had been opened to it, I could see it on many of the carved boulders around Thangboche, where before it had just been carving that I had been too lazy to try to read because it was unfamiliar. I wondered how many other secrets this land still held, just waiting for me to wake up and perceive them.

15

Undercurrents

At the risk of hurting Jangbu's feelings, I decided to invade
the kitchen and show him how to make sweet-and-sour sauce
in the hope of tempting Julie to eat. He took it very well,
watching carefully as I spooned in the ingredients. I hoped
he would not think it was a reflection on his cooking, which
really had been excellent, and in all conditions too. I ate stew
with the Sherpas. If I fished out the chillies before biting
into them, it was really quite tasty. Dawa returned with Julie's
plate almost untouched.

'She didn't eat it. I'll take some fruit.'

Jangbu said, 'Keep her talking and slip an extra spoonful
on while she's not looking.'

Dawa lumbered out again, ponderous in his layers of
clothes.

Outside, the gale began to gather force. Lhakpa peered
out at Ama Dablam, fading into the evening.

'There are going to be some expedition people killed if
this keeps up. It's always the same.'

I tried to imagine what this wind would be like up on
the ridge, and then decided I would rather not. The tent
flapped noisily all night. I wondered what Julie was thinking
about.

J ¶ Thank goodness I didn't have to walk anywhere today. I feel as if I have no control over my limbs and have no interest in what is going on around me. My physical needs are taking second place to an urgent need to try to regain my mental energy. I gave all I was capable of giving to make it to Kala Patthar. I feel so utterly drained of all feeling, as if it bled out of me on the way up that hill, and can't be gathered up again.

We were making quite good progress when suddenly my strength and energy deserted me. I had to rest every few yards and the rests were not doing me any good. No sooner were we up again than I was pleading for another stop. Elaine was very supportive, both morally and physically, but I was almost beyond caring what happened to either of us so long as this torture could be ended.

Long before the summit I was begging Elaine to let me go back. Yet deep down I knew that if I abandoned it then I could never face the climb again. I was stuck between wanting to go on for the guide dog appeal and feeling that, if I did, I would surely die of exhaustion. I never imagined it was possible to feel so totally exhausted and still be conscious, let alone moving. I kept myself going by sheer force of will, nothing else. It was unmitigated hell!

At the crown of the hill I was faced with a great tumble of boulders, a scramble I would have relished in normal circumstances. Instead it was just another interminable period of heaving and straining and being urged along, dazed, by the others. The Sherpas wanted to carry me to the top and down again, but even in the depths of my misery, I knew that this would hardly count in the eyes of my sponsors. I bless them for their concern. I knew that Elaine felt bad about the state I was in, but she also saw that I would never forgive myself if I did not achieve the goal. It is due in no small part to her understanding that I eventually got there at all. At the top I burst into uncontrollable tears of relief, which were soon forgotten in the unlooked-for hazard of vertigo. It must have been the effect of directing my eye-consciousness to where I knew there was an awful drop.

Posing for photographs was horrible. While trying to look cheerful and interested at the 'wonderful achievement', I was utterly consumed by the appalling thought of how we were ever going to get down again to Gorakche. When we finally staggered into camp I burst into tears of relief – for the third time that day. Even in my sleeping-bag I felt wretched, restless and uneasy, unable to concentrate on anything for more than a few seconds, more disorientated than I had ever been in my life before. I don't know if it was the altitude, exhaustion, the memory of the vertigo, or a combination of all of it.

It's hard for a blind person to be cut off from conversation and socialising at any time, but being left alone in the evenings here is making me feel anxious as well as lonely. Neither of us has mentioned getting on each other's nerves, but if this is Elaine's way of saying it, it is more hurtful by implication than in plain words. Though I keep telling myself she just assumes I want to be alone, I am beginning to wonder if the strain of taking on too much has irrevocably damaged our friendship.

Although not eating in itself doesn't bother me, my depressed mental state does, and of course they are tied up with each other. I wish I could make Elaine understand that the more she fusses, the less I can eat. I believe she is blaming herself for pushing me so near my limit. What worries me is that I don't seem to be able to get close enough to her emotionally to explain that I'm glad she helped me in the way she did. I know I'm being perverse in cutting myself off from her, but until I'm stronger again, I can't cope with another person's complexity. I end up feeling and showing irritation, and then being sorry for it. I'm locked up in a cage of black depression, and all I can think of is how annoying it is to have someone insisting I eat and drink when I don't even want to think about it, let alone do it.

I could have cut my tongue out when I told Elaine I had been anorexic, and then began to remember what it had been like. After the first few days I didn't feel ill. On the contrary, it was like being on a mild high all the time – an ethereal, other-worldly quality that can be as addictive as any drug. At that time I felt that my body was coasting along, making minimal demands on me while I was struggling to come to terms with the emotional upheaval of divorce. In the end, I had the same sense of reluctance in leaving the anorexia high behind, and making my body grow solid flesh again, that I had as a child in hospital, leaving the enticing light and returning to my body again. Perhaps having had a glimpse beyond death, I don't seem to feel the fear of it that is expected in our society.

The shock of physical and mental exhaustion has somehow cracked the veneer of superficiality I've been putting on everything. I have been skittering along on the surface, instinctively avoiding looking deeper, in order to concentrate on the summit. Putting that behind me leaves no further excuses for escapism. Suddenly I am forced to face up to problems I've been running from ever since leaving England. Have I been deluding myself with all my plans for living a single, independent life in a new area, with a new job, and so on? Kala Patthar had become a symbol for my other goals, but the fulfilment came as a nasty shock. I succeeded, yet I feel I failed to cope with it emotionally. Unless I understand myself, how can I be satisfied with outward success?

Now, with my attention focussing on home, I am even less capable of dealing with what is going on here, even though I realise the futility of trying to be in two places at once. ¶

Next morning we sat and waited while the crew made several attempts to reorganise the zopkio loads into workable loads for Kaji and Mingmar.

Julie suddenly broke the silence. 'I think I'm going home as soon as we get back to Kathmandu.'

'Why?'

'I never realised I'd feel so lonely and bored out here. You just go off with the others and leave me on my own.'

'What else am I supposed to do? Every time I come over to talk to you I just get snapped at and ignored. And you're nice to everyone else. I mean, I can take a hint.'

'Well, it would be nice to be asked over sometimes, to eat with everyone else.'

'I'm sorry. You certainly didn't give that impression. You always seemed to be tired and cold, totally pissed off with me, and you've always hated smoky fires and chillied stew.'

'Well, I'm sorry too. You're the last person I'd want to snap at and upset. I'm really just depressed and homesick, and missing my family. Always having to have someone with me is like being shackled. I feel so horribly constricted physically I can hardly bear it. A lot of it's just missing the constant physical contact with Bruno; when I'm at home he follows me around and edges up to me wherever I am. And I miss the physical warmth too . . . '

'You don't have him in the blankets with you, do you?'

'No, but I must confess I do have the cat in.'

'No wonder you need an expedition friend.'

'Actually, at home I have the cat *and* a hot-water-bottle! It's just that when you're down, you start to think of all the bad things that have happened in your life –'

'The ones you can conveniently forget about when you're feeling good –'

'They all come to the surface, and you start to wallow in them and feel really suicidal . . . if I'd come down to dinner I'd have just got fed up with the awful chillies and the smoke and not being able to understand the conversation . . . '

'Why don't you ask Lhakpa or Jangbu to teach you some Nepali? It's the easiest topic of conversation when you're a bit stuck for the language.'

'Okay, I will. Think positive. And I'm going to drink the place dry today.'

Suddenly we were both laughing, mainly with relief. The dead-lock was broken. Then I noticed something else to laugh at.

'You know those horns Tawa sold to Lhakpa? Well, they've

tied a huge load for Kaji with the horns crowning the top; three of them are heaving him to his feet – and off he goes. I don't know if he looks more like a yak or a Viking!'

There was a roar of laughter from our irrepressible crew, and a passable imitation of a yak grunt from Kaji, before he staggered off down the road.

We didn't quite make it to Khumjung that day. Julie had begun to eat and drink again, but still her strength needed some time to return. We made camp by a little tea-shop at the bottom of the last hill into Khumjung. The fire was in an inner room, so Julie and I sat in the outer room to drink tea. It was smokeless but cold, and I caught myself suffering small pangs of regret when the crew were invited to sit round the fire and eat potatoes and chilli. If I had been alone they would have invited me too, but they knew Julie did not like the smoke – or the chilli. I argued with myself that you can't have everything, and it was a small price to pay to have Julie back on speaking terms again.

There was a sudden invasion of people into the tea-shop, big people with big voices and personalities immediately filling the room with boisterous laughter and demands for chang. It was part of the expedition from Ama Dablam, abandoning their attempt because of the high winds. The atmosphere became animated with epic stories of gale-force winds and ropes being damaged by falling stones.

'So we decided to bag it while we were still in one piece. My brother and his wife are still up there packing the last of the things out of Base Camp.'

Jangbu whispered, 'If he knew about hot-water-bottles he wouldn't have had to bring his wife.'

'Shh! Shuttup!'

The story continued, ranging from Pema's nightmares and stay in Base Camp to the high winds that blew rocks off the top of the ridge. The young Canadian was trying hard to keep up with the macho display of the older man, and a slightly competitive atmosphere developed. They ordered more chang.

Lhakpa said, in Nepali so as not to offend the climbers, 'I

went to the top of Ama Dablam a couple of years ago with a
French team. It's not that hard. I don't know why they didn't
wait in Base Camp till the wind dropped.'

I wondered if the competitiveness was beginning to affect
him too.

'No bad dreams?'

'Not me! Pema's a friend of mine. I met up with him in
Namche Bazar before he left and he asked me to come along
as climbing Sherpa with him to Ama Dablam. But when I got
to Lukla there was a message from Brian saying I had to go
to Paphlu to meet two girls off the plane.'

'What *would* you have done when Pema had his dreams?'

'I'd have tucked him up in Base Camp and gone to the
top again.'

The chang was flowing very freely now, and the verbal
muscle-flexing was in full sway. The two Sherpas running the
tea-shop were joining in, angling the conversation around
to the possibilities of employment on the climbers' next
expedition.

Lhakpa looked the men up and down critically.

'Their clothes are really old and worn. They don't look
the kind to give good equipment to their staff. Italians and
Germans usually give the most. And the best stuff.'

I smiled as I remembered how Shona knew all the brand
names and prices of every item of equipment from a dozen
different countries. Western consumerism had been late
arriving in Nepal, but now it was taking hold fast. I
knew many of the lamas had harsh things to say about it,
that it was turning their people away from their spiritual
path. I still held the hope that their strong spiritual background would help at least some of them to keep it in pro-
portion, rather than let it take over their lives completely.
In some situations I would regard this as no more than foolish
optimism, yet at times like this, I found I had renewed faith in
that optimism. Here was Lhakpa eyeing up the 'baksheesh'
potential of this expedition – yet, at the same time, I had
already told them all at the beginning that the equipment
they had been given was all the baksheesh they were going to

get. We did not have enough money to give them a cash tip as well at the end of the trek. In spite of that, they had gone out of their way to give us extra help along every step of the journey – even to the point of carrying Julie rather than have us spend money we could ill afford on a riding yak. So what was in it for them? My mind went back to the row of offering-bowls in the temple, and Tapkhay's voice – 'It is not that the Buddhas need what we offer; they are beyond all that. But it is good for our minds to make the offerings.' To carry the essence of the practice into everyday life with ordinary human beings is to give whatever you can, simply because it is a good thing to do: to be able to see beyond the obvious benefits to the recipient or the possible material rewards to the giver. I still felt I could perceive an element of this vision among the tremendous changes the people here were undergoing.

It was getting cold. The climbers left, and we went back to the tents. The wind had eased, and the night was quiet.

It was only a short climb to Khumjung in the morning. Kaji passed us, like a two-legged pantomime yak. Further on we caught up with Mingmar wrestling with the great Red Sausage.

'I think I'll leave it here and carry Julie instead!'

I helped him steady the thing while he sorted out the balance of it. Even with something that size to carry, he still made better time up the hill than we did.

Tsingdrolma was walking around the chörten with two old women from the village. They were holding rosaries and reciting mantras as they walked.

Tsingdrolma turned to greet us.

'*Namaste!* Did you have a good journey? Our Tawa came back and said Julie had been up to Kala Patthar! You must come back and have some tea with me.'

We followed her to her house, while she told the story to her two friends. They nodded and clicked their tongues, then waved and left us to go back to their homes.

We sat down in the one room of the little hotel while Tsingdrolma made the tea. On the wall was a poster for an

Everest expedition of twelve years ago. I looked through
the photographs of the members. Almost half of them had
since been killed in the mountains. It was strange to see
them together again. Next to the poster was a photograph
of Tsingdrolma's son, with the climber from Ama Dablam,
on a previous expedition. Tucked behind the photograph was
the son's certificate from the climbing course held in Nepal to
train expedition employees. Lhakpa was reading through the
certificate, trying to decipher the signatures at the bottom.

'I might be going on this course next summer. Ongdi says
he thinks it's a good idea. Having the certificate can get you
on to the big-money expeditions more easily.'

'I thought you didn't do it any more.'

'Well, you know, maybe just once or twice, if the money's
really good.'

Suddenly I felt sad. There would always be the temptation
to risk it just one more time for that kind of money, and the
odds were so short. These villages lose a few every year; it is
becoming part of the new culture. I tried not to think of the
chörtens on the mountain above.

Tsingdrolma walked part of the way up to Kunde with
us. The crew were already ensconced in a grassy field with a
stone hut in one corner. I soon discovered the attraction of
this spot; the hut was to be the cook-shelter, but because it
was also occupied by a local family there would be a fire
round which to keep warm in the evening. We decided to stay
here for two days. Julie needed to recoup her strength, and
there was not enough time left to get to Lawudo as we had
originally planned, because of the several days spent on an
unplanned detour to Thumbuk. We had visited one monastery
instead of another, and it seemed a fair trade as far as the
itinerary was concerned. As far as we were concerned, the
time with Tapkhay had been one of the happiest of the whole
trip. We were both looking forward to seeing him again in
Kathmandu.

It was a lazy couple of days, in which we took delight in
mundane chores like laundry and hair-washing – only the
second opportunity of the trek for the latter. The secret is to

do it early and sit in the sun, or else your hair will freeze on your head. Julie was feeling much better, and had changed her mind about going home when we reached Kathmandu.

J ¶ I can hardly believe my diary of the last few days. But I won't erase it. The psychologists will have a field day with all that negativity. I woke this morning feeling as if a great load had been lifted off my mind. I'll see if Elaine wants me along at the end of the trek. If she does, I'll stay, because I'm sure I'll regret it later if I don't. If she thinks she's had enough I can't blame her.

I've noticed that although the altitude seems to play havoc with my appetite, the air is so clear and clean here I have had no headaches at all, apart from the small one in Namche. At home in London I have so many headaches . . .

I do enjoy the simplicity of the Sherpa sense of humour. This morning they announced that we would be camping at the Alpine Lodge below Namche tomorrow. Elaine said they must put up the loo tent, as I wouldn't use the toilets because of the smell. They thought it was hilarious that someone should be so picky, and asked how on earth we were going to manage in India. Jangbu said we'd have to take a loo tent with us, and a Sherpa to put it up every day! I can just see us trying to do that in Delhi. I think they appreciate us laughing at ourselves. They thought it very funny when I started imitating the way I'd been on Kala Patthar, staggering around clutching my stomach, and moaning, 'I can't go on! I can't go on!' But we have caught them out too. In the absence of telephones they have acquired the habit of hailing each other from a distance: 'Oi!'—to which the reply is 'Ah!' We've told them that as these are the only two words in the Sherpa language, we too can speak it fluently, and have begun to echo them every time they do it. Now they are so self-conscious about it they start to giggle even before we can tease them. ¶

That evening Jangbu came over to my tent.
'There's chang in the kitchen.'

It was getting far too cold to be able to write in a diary, I told myself. I went to see Julie.

'There's chang in the kitchen.'

'And Julie's in her sleeping-bag. I think I'll give the smoke and chillies a miss tonight. You go.'

'So long as you don't mind.'

'Not in these temperatures.'

'You should get your dressing-gown and slippers on. Take a tip from the ravens.'

'Is that what you've done?'

'Not quite. Just everything I possess. In layers.'

'I'll stick with the sleeping-bag, thank you.'

The stone hut was crowded and dark, the fire shining red-orange on hands and faces as everyone gathered about its meagre warmth. The jug of chang was passing round, and each in turn would go through the pretence of refusal before accepting. The two men nearest the fire were returning home from an expedition, flashing their new gear, and obviously with money in their pockets. They were engaged in an elaborate word-play in Nepali, to impress their stay-at-home neighbours with their competence in a second language.

A lean, muscular man in his forties was sitting quietly in the corner, smoking and watching the performance. There was nothing remarkable about his appearance, yet he stood out from the crowd by the very aloofness and assurance of his manner.

Lhakpa said, 'That's Sundare. He's been to the top of Everest three times. Now he doesn't climb. He's working for the tourist board.'

Lhakpa was becoming distracted by Sundare's cigarette.

'Maybe just one?'

'If you have one you'll start again.'

Jangbu came over, looking concerned. 'Where's your chewing-gum? I'll get it for you.'

Sundare leaned over and offered Lhakpa a cigarette.

'No, it's okay. I don't smoke.'

The conversation had shifted to past adventures and ex-peditions. One of the men had been over the passes east of

Ama Dablam, and was describing the route through. It seemed to alternate between snow-covered passes and dense jungles swarming with leeches.

'No food available for seventeen days till you get across to the Arun. It's a long time since I went there. Nobody goes there much.'

It was an area I had always wanted to explore. There was a legend that the hidden valley of Khembalung lay somewhere in those mountains, invisible to all without the spiritual attainments with which to perceive it. Only powerful yogins and lamas could enter it, and from it there was no return. Even so, I had always felt a strange curiosity about it, although now I did not have the courage to ask the speaker if he knew anything about the valley.

I walked back to the tents. In the sunset the mountains faded from gold to purple. I wondered what lay beyond.

Lhakpa was coughing the next morning and Julie offered him the bottle of cough-mixture she was no longer using.

'It's pretty strong, so he should stick to small doses.'

'Okay. Did you hear that Lhakpa? Only a small bit at a time.'

Lhakpa sniffed the bottle, then took it without a deal of enthusiasm. It was similar to the cough-mixture available in all the little shops in Nepal, but much stronger.

We made our way slowly down the steep hill to Namche, as Julie's foot was still painful in spite of the bandage.

'Oh no.'

'What?'

'The dog coming up the hill with these trekkers looks alarmingly familiar.'

It recognised us and came scampering over, black and white plumed tail waving over its back. It made straight for Julie and rubbed itself around her legs.

'Oh look, isn't it friendly!'

'If you play with it and make a fuss of it like that we'll never get rid of it.'

'Oh, I know, but it's so *sweet*!'

'Don't you dare complain about it when it keeps you

awake all night then. The other trekkers have already gone on without it.'

'Oh, all right then.'

The dog followed us all the way down the hill.

'Oh dear. I won't fuss it any more. We'll have to make it go away somehow.'

Lhakpa looked round. 'You don't want it?' He picked up a pebble and threw it at the dog. It snarled and went for him, snapping at his ankles. I drew back instinctively at this sudden change of character.

Julie was shouting. 'Stop it! I will *not* have it! I will *not* have animals hurt.'

Suddenly I was angry.

'It's not fair. It's not fair to encourage it till it follows us, then go all holier-than-thou with the Sherpas when they have to get rid of it for you. You complained more than anyone when it kept you awake, so why do you insist on creating the situation in the first place?'

'All right. You've said your bit.'

We walked on in silence. I was as surprised by my outburst as she was. I had not realised I was as involved as that. I had wanted to play with the dog too, and it had been hard to refrain just because of the consequences, not just for us, but for it also. It also upset me. I didn't like to see animals hurt either, and now it was left to me to solve the problem.

We reached Namche and went into one of the bigger Sherpa hotels for tea. The dog came too. Then we managed to shut it in and sneak off down the hill. I felt sorry for the next group of trekkers who would go in there and leave with a canine problem trotting along behind. The squabble was left behind with the dog. In spite of Julie's sore foot, it was a slow but pleasant meander down the zig-zags to the bridge.

Lhakpa had been ahead of us for a while. We came upon him around a corner, asleep on a large rock.

'Hey, wake up Lhakpa! That's the second time you've been asleep this morning.'

He sat up slowly, shaking his head as if to clear it.

'Are you all right?'

'Very sleepy. And I can see two of you.'

'How much of that cough medicine did he have?' Julie asked.

'How much was there?'

'Over half a bottle.'

'Oh my God. Lhakpa. Oi! Wake up! How much did you drink?'

'All of it. You said all of it.'

'I said a *small bit*, not *all of it*! Oh, no; what other dreadful things are likely to happen to him?'

'Um . . . sleepiness, dizziness, probably very thirsty and liable to do daft things.'

'He doesn't need an overdose of cough medicine to do daft things. I suppose he'll survive. I'll just have to keep an eye on him, to make sure he doesn't fall off the trail.'

Lhakpa took a perverse delight in convincing me he was about to do something irrevocably stupid every five minutes or so.

'You're almost being daft enough to be back to normal. If you're going to consume any more noxious substances and scare me half to death, let me know first next time.'

'Wasn't my fault. How am I supposed to read German?'

'You must have the constitution of a yak. Anyone else would have been comatose on that lot.'

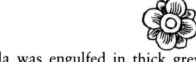

Lukla was engulfed in thick grey cloud when we reached it the following day. We sat in the cookshelter drinking tea and formulating alternative plans.

'This cloud could clear tomorrow or after two weeks. There hasn't been a flight for five days already because of the high winds,' I told Julie.

'I'm not sure about walking all the way out with my foot the way it is.'

'We haven't got time for that anyway, before our flight out from Kathmandu.'

Lhakpa said, 'My brother's got a horse. I could go to

Pang Kwam Ma and fetch it. With Julie riding, we could walk out in time.'

'Okay. If there's no flight tomorrow, you go and get the horse, and we'll meet you the other side of that icy part of the trail. It would be too dangerous to ride that stretch anyway.'

'Sounds quite exciting! I don't think I'll mind so much if the plane doesn't come after all.'

We spent the afternoon at Phurba's house, drinking tea and watching the clouds outside the window roll in thicker by the minute. Every so often Lhakpa and I would walk down to the Royal Nepal Airlines office to see if it had opened for seat confirmation. A straggly queue had formed outside, mainly Sherpas and Tibetans, with a few trekkers fidgeting impatiently in the clammy cold. The office manager finally arrived, bustling and cheerful in spite of the weather.

We crowded into the small stone-built room with its creaking plank floor and chipped tubular steel chairs. A couple of posters were sellotaped to the wall – Annapurna with poinsettia in the foreground and alpenglow on the summit. 'RNAC. Flight to Enchantment.' A notice above the manager's desk said in English: 'Due to unfavourable mountain weather conditions flights may be delayed for extended periods. Passengers deciding to walk out are requested to inform this office. With extensive overbooking after long delays, uplift of passengers cannot be guaranteed.'

Lhakpa wormed his way back from the front of the crowd looking pleased with himself. We were on the first flight out tomorrow if the plane came.

The next morning dawned still, crisp and clear; the plane came, and we were uplifted.

Only Lhakpa and Jangbu were returning to Kathmandu to look for more work. Dawa, Kaji and Mingmar were going home. They would walk from Lukla and be there in less than a day. Dawa had shambled over as we waited by the gate, kataks in his hands and tears in his eyes.

'Goodbye, good luck!' He turned and clumped away.

I always find goodbyes hard.

Lhakpa pushed boarding-cards into our hands and manoeuvred us onto the plane. After the initial terrifying rush down the sloping dirt runway we were off the end, high over the deep gorge of the Dudh Kosi. The winds were still strong over the Lamijura, so we followed the river south until we could turn westwards along the course of the Sun Kosi. The hills were lower here, and the force of the wind less concentrated on the passes.

The forests in this region have suffered even more extensively than the forests of Solu-Khumbu. The hills below lay stripped and bare, dry winter grass interspersed with bare earth, a faded brown with only the occasional dark green patch of low scrub. Every hill was scored deep with white erosion runnels, as if clawed by some giant cat. The land of enchantment was dying, as surely as the monsoon would come and pour its water back to the sea. But the pain of Nepal is only a small part of the problem suffered over the whole surface of the earth. While the superpowers build arsenals to protect themselves from jealous neighbours, the life of their homeland is running out from beneath their feet.

16

Elephant

Kathmandu seemed incredibly noisy and crowded, the air heavy with petrol fumes. Lhakpa and Jangbu helped us to move our things over to Samten's house in Boudnath, just outside the city. It was a relief to be out of the traffic – so little compared to England, yet so frenetic after the streams and pine forests of Solu-Khumbu.

Samten was delighted to see us, in spite of the fact that her sister was visiting from Darjeeling and the house was already swarming with children. Three of them came bundling out of one of the rooms as we entered, hanging onto our hands and climbing over us. Samten was very pregnant now, smiling a welcome and trying to clear the kids away from under our feet. We sat on a rug-covered bed in her front room while she brought tea, stepping carefully over a couple of crawling infants.

'How many children have you got here today?'

'Well, there are my two, and my sister from Darjeeling has four; then my brother's here for the day as well, and he's got three.' She laughed. 'And when they come to visit next year there'll be one more! I didn't plan to have any more, but the contraceptive injections were giving me headaches and dizziness, so I had to stop them.'

I knew that some of the medications available out here would not pass the safety regulations in the West.

Samten tried on the baby-carrier. 'Yes, it's a good fit. Now I can get on with my work when the baby comes.'

'You always carried them in a blanket before – why the change?'

'Oh, you carry them in a blanket and they're more likely to fall out! This is better. Keeps them in.'

Samten and her husband worked long hours in the little carpet business they ran from their house; all but three rooms were full of balls of coloured wool, looms and rugs. Julie spent the rest of the afternoon choosing a rug to take home. Although I had to describe the colours to her, she was able to feel every detail of the pattern because each colour had been trimmed with scissors to stand out from the background.

We ate noodle soup with the family, then slept early in the front room by the household altar. The next day would be a hectic scramble, making travel arrangements.

We took a taxi into the city. The bus would have been one rupee instead of twenty, but when it came to it I couldn't face the crush.

In Thamel we ran into Lindsay, his six-foot frame unmistakable among the small Nepalese. He looked happier after his trek and was going home within a few days. With Scottish thrift, he was travelling overland to Delhi, and had words of warning about Indian visas.

'Give it plenty of time. Ye'll have to queue for at least three hours at the Embassy, to take it in and to pick it up. And y'need a letter from the British Consulate. Get that first or they'll send you out to queue all over again. And ye'll both have to go in person.'

'Ugh. What a way to spend your holidays. Still, thanks for the warning.'

It took us a while to locate the Sajha Medical Hall which was the place recommended to get Julie's foot X-rayed. It was just a doorway off the main street, with a sign above it. Inside was a dark room with an X-ray machine looking rather incongruous on its own in the middle of the cement floor. However, it produced perfectly adequate pictures of Julie's foot which we took to the Canadian clinic at the other side of town. The doctor was reassuring: he diagnosed no broken bones, perhaps a sprain. At least it gave us an excuse to travel by taxi or rickshaw for the rest of the day. The next stop was the Ongdi Trekking office, where Brian was trying to balance bills and receipts, and get his passport renewed for a trip to Europe, all at the same time. I left messages for Lhakpa and Jangbu to come for a meal with us that evening. They both had been given new jobs and would be leaving town very shortly.

Ang Dorjee's widow was waiting in the main office. She sat quietly, her eyes cast down. She had come down from Khumbu to find out about the insurance money, most of which would go to pay back what she would have borrowed for Dorjee's funeral puja. The rest, she and the four children would try to live on.

I left Julie there and did the rounds, making sure all our travel arrangements were in order, both for Tiger Tops and for the flight out. On our previous visit to Kathmandu I had helped a young Tibetan friend, Dakpa, with his arrangements to travel to England, where he was to work on some translations of Tibetan manuscripts. I had come to the conclusion it would be better if he travelled with us. Although intelligent and well-educated, he seemed to have a mental block as far as dates and schedules were concerned, and I had visions of him disappearing somewhere between Kathmandu and Heathrow. He had agreed to meet us at Samten's the day we arrived back from Lukla, but there had been no sign of him. If he didn't find us soon, I would have to go looking for him.

We headed for Narayani's, calling at Shona's on the way to return the sunglasses. Tapkhay was there. Kathmandu is like that: you always bump into people you know as if it were a tiny village instead of a capital city.

'Hello! I was going to find you tomorrow.'

'We're going to eat. Coming?'

We passed a bearded American in the entrance to the restaurant. He looked familiar, so I smiled and said hello. After I had gone past, I realised who it was.

'Stefan! What are you doing here?'

'My girlfriend arrived a little early. I must have gotten a later flight out the same day as you.'

Unexpectedly the meal had turned into a party, with seven of us. Jangbu was already waiting, and a minute later Lhakpa clumped in, rucksack on his back and a bunch of ice-screws dangling from his belt.

'What on earth are you doing with that lot?'

'Big display tomorrow for King's birthday. They've built a model of Everest in Ratna Park, and want some Sherpas to demonstrate climbing it with gear. Big honour. For King. Pay's good too.'

'What will they think of next?'

'I'll let you know.' He stashed the gear in the corner and sat down.

We must have looked an odd assortment. Stefan and I looked more or less like lower-income tourists, while his girl-friend, a black American and a highly qualified doctor, was very glamorous. Tapkhay was his usual beaming cheerful self, quite distinctive with his red robes and shaven head. Julie was trying to look like an Indian tonight, wearing a Punjabi smock and baggy pants she had bought in the market, with a long woolly pigtail braided into her hair. Jangbu still looked about sixteen, although Lhakpa assured me he was twenty-two. Lhakpa himself appeared ready to bivouac halfway up Everest. But then, at Narayani's, no one takes much notice of anything, so long as you can eat enormous quantities of food in a confined space. Julie and I were experiencing the tremendous increase in appetite that always occurs when you have been at altitude for a while and then descend. It is as if your system suddenly wakes up and remembers what food is all about. Julie, of course, had been eating so little that the effects now were dramatic. She found it impossible to wait for the main course, and had to have a quick slice of chocolate cake to keep her strength up until it came. Jangbu was having a wonderful time teasing her and urging her on to greater efforts.

'I hope he's not offended that I never ate as much of his food as this.'

'He doesn't seem to be.'

We arrived back at Samten's late and made an attempt at packing up the things we would not need in a jungle. We should have had much less now we were minus the food and extra equipment, but Julie had been shopping in the bazar and had become a little over-enthusiastic. The Red and Blue Sausages were full again.

'May I remind you of something you once said about hating Christmas shopping?'

'Oh, I know, but everything's so *nice*. It's impossible to choose!'

There was still no sign of Dakpa. I decided to walk up to his house early the next morning, before our flight to Chitwan and the Tiger Tops lodge.

Ambling through the old part of the city in the early hours of the morning, I found that I was falling in love with Kathmandu all over again. Despite the pollution that is creeping in, and the disillusionment I sometimes felt at the encroaching commercialism, I could see again facets of the unchanged pace of life weaving through it all.

Women were coming out of their houses carrying polished brass plates of marigolds, rice, and red tika powder to offer at one of the many Hindu shrines on every street. The statues on the shrines were already red with the powder, and surrounded by a scattering of rice and marigolds. The shopkeepers were opening their shutters and pulling out their wares from the dark interiors. Vegetable sellers were scrubbing up their produce, calling out to the Newari porters carrying fresh stock, Chinese style, in baskets suspended from a shoulder pole. A butcher was arranging cuts of mutton on a slab, the skin dyed yellow with turmeric, bright against the pink flesh.

'Good morning madam. Why not buy some good mutton? Then you will have meat and we will have money!'

I laughed and waved and walked on.

Dakpa was having breakfast: salt tea and tsampa, no extras.

'I was going to come and see you today.'

'We're flying to Chitwan today.'

We walked back to the city together. I still could not tell if he had really grasped our dates, times, and schedules. One minute we seemed to be communicating, the next he was far away in a world of his own. I decided to give him the tickets and instructions on where to meet us on our return from Chitwan, and to hope for the best.

Our previous time together had been spent around the ancient temples and shrines of the Kathmandu valley. Dakpa's store of knowledge and stories about these places, and the people and gods who had been there before, seemed limitless. Given plenty of time and quiet, his soft poet's voice would weave pictures and stories of a time long past, bringing life and meaning to the crumbling stone by which we stood. I wondered what he would make of England.

The quiet dirt streets gave way to the noise and traffic of the city centre. Dakpa was looking around silently. It was impossible to tell what he was thinking. Finally he spoke.

'I was in Kathmandu ten years ago. It has changed very much since then. I once knew a German who came every year to visit the city. He would always go and look at a beautiful carved window in one of the old houses. Then, last year, he came and they had torn out the old window and put in a big new modern window. He said to me, "I will not come back now. The window is gone. There is nothing for me here."'

He offered no opinion or comment on the story, nor did he expect any.

We walked on in silence. I knew he had spent many years in a monastery and was used to thinking more than he spoke.

I barely made it back in time for the plane. It was a wonderful relief to be travelling with only a small daypack of toiletries and spare underwear for two nights in tropical jungle, with no camping.

Julie became excited before the elephants even appeared.

'I've always wanted to ride an elephant. It's just another of my childhood ambitions.'

'I'm getting a bit wary of your childhood ambitions. Elephants and camels are one thing, but when you start telling me you want to cuddle a snake and stroke a tiger . . . '

The elephants came round the corner, slow and ponderous, trunks swaying with their steps. They knelt, so that passengers could climb into the wooden seats on their backs. It took two hours through the jungle to reach the lodge. I tore off passing leaves so that Julie could build up a picture of the jungle we were in. We passed a rhino in the river. I took photographs, then grabbed Julie's legs as she leaned over to capture a disgruntled snort on tape. Later, there was time for a short walk with one of the naturalists, Julie's fingers finding their way into tiger pug marks and exploring a tall termite nest.

'How would you feel if someone stuck their finger down your air-conditioning system?'

'I'm hoping there's nobody at home.'

Afterwards we sat in the lodge drinking tea. Now it was my turn to feel at a loss, aimless, unable to become engaged in anything. I had focussed all my attention and energy, not so much on Kala Patthar as on getting us down again in one piece. It is always like this at the end of an expedition. Once beyond the point of focus, you find yourself in the vacuum left by all that spent energy. Wherever you are, and whatever you are doing afterwards, there seems to be a kind of distance, a lack of involvement.

One of the guests was the personnel officer of a large company. She was interested in the sponsored walk and the guide dogs. When Julie had finished explaining, the woman turned to me.

'Have you worked with the blind very much before?'

I felt Julie stiffen with indignation, but she saved her comments until the woman was out of earshot.

'Ooh! It always hits you harder when it comes from some intelligent and well-educated. Handicapped people couldn't possibly have *friends*, could they? Just social workers! I wonder why it is the Sherpas and Tibetans can respond so much more naturally. It was so refreshing for me. Do you remember when Samten suddenly asked, "Does being blind make you sad?" Back home, it's more often old people and children who can relate like that – more accepting and less embarrassed.'

We sat with a group of Australians at supper. One of the men thought he had met us before.

'Are you sure you haven't been in Australia recently?' Eventually he remembered he had seen the rock-climbing film: the BBC must have sold it to Australian television.

Julie said she hoped it would all help the dog appeal as Australia had its own Guide Dog Association. That day in Derbyshire seemed so long ago now. So did Kala Patthar, when I came to think of it. The only tangible reminder here was Julie's appetite. It had levelled out in Kathmandu, but we had since descended another four and a half thousand feet to Tiger Tops, and it reasserted itself all over again. The Australians gave her a round of applause after the fifth helping of apple crumble and cream.

Lisa Van Gruisen arrived, with a glittering crowd of film people.

'We're having a bit of a celebration – Pamela Bellwood's getting married tomorrow – ' She stopped at my blank look. 'Don't you watch any television?'

·'Not really.'

'She's one of the stars of "Dynasty". It's the most popular soap opera currently running. Come over and have a drink.'

They had all had a three-hour start on us, and in any case their conversation revolved around a different world. The film-star had a hollow-eyed, exhausted kind of beauty, which suddenly made her look very young and vulnerable amongst all the gloss and professionalism.

We stayed a while, then made our apologies and went back to the lodge. Julie made straight for bed.

'What's this?' She rummaged around inside the bed for a minute, before pulling out a hot-water-bottle. 'Look, there's even an expedition friend waiting for us! Good idea too; I thought the jungle would be a lot hotter than this, even in winter.' She wriggled under the covers. 'Plain English will never be the same again. Expedition friends, ravens wearing their dressing-gowns and slippers, "No problem!" the answer to almost everything . . . I wonder what new language we'll invent next.'

We lay awake and chatted, toes curled round hot-water-bottles. Julie's thoughts were turning to home – to Bruno, to her parents, to the new house she was hoping to buy outside London. It was too soon for me to find fresh mental energies for new directions. I was still in a kind of limbo, living with the images of what had gone before. I listened for a while, but soon fell asleep.

Dawn brings a heavy mist to the jungle, dripping through the trees like a soft rain. The elephants stood waiting in the hazy green shadows, grey hulks among the wet leaves. We had felt their wrinkled skin and warm, chapatti-like ears, listened to them blowing softly down their trunks. Without Julie it would have been a different jungle, a different city, a different mountain. One of the joys of being with her was her total, childlike delight in the fresh things I could find to show her, which made it easy to accept that she would have correspond-ing swings in mood when things did not go well. I knew for her this chapter of her life was drawing to a close. Once we returned home she would be busy with her new plans and we would see little of each other. It was hard not to feel disappointed. I found myself wanting what we had been through together to mean more to her. Yet, even through the sense of loss, I could see she was right to pursue her own life, and this would in no way invalidate what we had done and experienced together. It was easy to fall into the trap of wanting to own part of someone – as impossible as trying to grasp at the essence of our adventure by hoarding the celluloid images from my camera. The adventure was the truth of an experience for two people at that time, and time moves on.

What had we really been trying to do? Perhaps we could never be quite sure. Raising money, maybe making a statement about blind people, maybe looking for something within ourselves. Whatever it was, I knew it would be foolish to try to cling to it. It was good to have done it. Now let it go.

High above in the dripping forest, a bird was singing.

Select Bibliography

This is less a list of references than a suggested book list for readers of *The Windhorse* who might like to discover more about places and themes touched on in recounting our own adventures.

Anderson, John G. (ed.): *Nepal* (an 'Insight Guide'), APA Publications, Singapore, 1985 (distributed by Harrap)

Blum, Arlene: *Annapurna, a Woman's Place*, Granada, London, 1980

Bonington, Chris: *Everest, the Hard Way*, Hodder & Stoughton, London, 1976

Bzruchka, Stephen, *A Guide to Trekking in Nepal*, The Mountaineers, Seattle, 1981

Dickinson, Leo: *Filming the Impossible*, Jonathan Cape, London, 1982

Gibbons, Bob, and Bob Ashford: *The Himalayan Kingdoms, Nepal, Bhutan and Sikkim*, Batsford, London, 1983

Gill, Linda: *Living High* (the story of a family trek in Nepal), Hodder & Stoughton, London, 1984

Hillary, Edmund: *Nothing Venture, Nothing Win* (autobiography), Hodder & Stoughton, London, 1975

Kelsang Gyatso, Geshe: *Buddhism in the Tibetan Tradition*, Routledge & Kegan Paul, London, 1984

Kelsang Gyatso, Geshe: *Meaningful to Behold*, Tharpa Publications, Conishead Priory, Ulverston, Cumbria, 1985

Mehta, Ashvin, and Maurice Herzog: *Himalaya: Encounters with Eternity*, Thames & Hudson, London, 1985

Napier, John: *Bigfoot: the Yeti and Sasquatch in Myth and Reality*, Jonathan Cape, London, 1972

Raj, P. A.: *Kathmandu and the Kingdom of Nepal*, Lonely Planet, Australia, 1983

Tulku, Tarthang: *Skilful Means*, Dharma Press, Everyville, California, 1978

Tenzin Gyatso, the Fourteenth Dalai Lama: *The Buddhism of Tibet*, Allen & Unwin, London, 1975

Unsworth, Walt: *Everest* (a history to 1980), Allen Lane, London, 1981

Von Fürer-Haimendorf, Christoph: *The Sherpas of Nepal: Buddhist Highlanders*, East-West Publications, London, 1979

Acknowledgements

We would like to thank British Airways and Tony Powell, and the Royal Nepal Airlines Corporation and Mr Pradhan for their assistance with air travel. Thanks are also due to the following for supplying us with excellent equipment for the expedition: Adidas, Gunter Pfau and Heidi Graf for boots, shoes and tracksuits; Blacks Alpine, Alan Day and Tony Morgan for rainsuits, rucksacks, sleeping-bags and tents; Campbell Dixon and John Strafford for Swiss Army knives; Damart Thermawear and J. Robson for thermal underwear; Europasport and Mike Jardine for socks and rope; Pentax and Peter Cox for cameras; Salewa and Hermann Huber for tents. Also much appreciated was the supply of dried foods from the following companies: Batchelors (Cup-a-Soup); Bovril (Marmite and Oxo cubes); Burtons (Gold Medal biscuits); Dornay Foods (Yeoman Mash); Jordan's (Original Crunchy Cereal); Johnson & Johnson (first aid and toiletries); Kelloggs (Rise and Shine drink); KP Foods (mixed nuts and raisins); Rowntree-Mackintosh (Yorkie Bars and Fruit Pastilles); Whitworth's Holdings (dried vegetables).

For generous support and help we should also like to thank Rick Donnelly, Peter Hatton, Alison Roberts, Joan Roberts and Sheila Smith, as well as the Royal National Institute for the Blind.